RELIGIOUS VOCATION--ITS JURIDIC CONCEPT

A Historical Synopsis and a Commentary

The Catholic University of America
Canon Law Studies
No. 328

RELIGIOUS VOCATION
ITS JURIDIC CONCEPT
A Historical Synopsis and a Commentary

A Dissertation
Submitted to the Faculty of the School of Canon Law of
the Catholic University of America in Partial
Fulfillment of the Requirements for the
Degree of Doctor of Canon Law

By the
REVEREND NORMAN F. McFARLAND, A.B., J.C.L.
Priest of the Archdiocese of San Francisco

The Catholic University of America Press
Washington, D. C.
1953

NIHIL OBSTAT:

Hieronymus D. Hannan, A.M., LL.B., S.T.D., J.C.D.
Censor Deputatus.

Washingtonii, D. C., die 17 maii, 1952

IMPRIMATUR:

Joannes J. Mitty, D.D.
Archiepiscopus Sancti Francisci

Sancti Francisci, die 20 maii, 1952.

IN MEMORY OF ALAN

TABLE OF CONTENTS

FOREWORD

To raise the question of religious vocation today is to invite controversial discussion. Is a call to the religious life something internal, or is it external? Is it divine, ecclesiastical, or a combination of both? Is it given to all men, at least in a relative sense, or is it given only to the special subjects of God's predilection? And what answer is to be given to those who ask: "But how am I to know if I am really called to the religious life? How can I be sure that this is the will of God for me?" These and similar questions have resulted in such a diversity of answers among contemporary authors that the whole question has become clouded with doubt and confusion.

It is with the purpose of clearing away the confusion by presenting the essential problem in bold relief and setting forth the legislator's *practical* answer that this study is undertaken. As the title indicates, the juridical point of view is emphasized. It is hoped that it will be of some value to all who are called upon to give a discerning answer to the age-old question, "Have I a religious vocation?" and that the presentation of speculative theological controversies in the light of legal realities will be of additional aid to those whose proper province it is directly to examine those subjects.

The writer welcomes this occasion to acknowledge his gratitude to the Most Reverend John J. Mitty, D.D., Archbishop of San Francisco, for the opportunity of advanced study in Canon Law at The Catholic University of America; to the members of the Faculty of the School of Canon Law for their guidance and their helpful direction; and to all others whose assistance and encouragement have contributed towards the completion of this work.

PART I
Preliminary

CHAPTER I
A STATEMENT OF POSITION

To isolate one section of being and to make it the object of intensified study is a valid procedure in the process of learning and can lead to a valuable increase of knowledge. But such procedure is not also without its intellectual difficulties. Experience has shown that concentrated study of isolated subjects, while adding greatly to man's fund of information about them, has at times resulted in gravely distorted concepts not only about the very subjects under examination, but in cognate fields of learning as well, and this because the part has been viewed independently of its relationship to the whole. For it is a plain fact that man does not know anything at all until he sees it in its context, that is, in its place in the totality to which it belongs. The part is not the whole, and unless one knows the whole, he does not know even the part.

This is true of all things whatsoever: it is true, therefore, of any study of religious vocation. It has become increasingly evident to the writer in the course of preparing this dissertation that much of the confusion that has risen in the past, and still abounds, concerning vocation to the religious state is due largely to a failure on the part of many to recognize this fundamental principle in their attempts to determine the nature of "the call" to that state. A work, for example, which treats the theology of religious vocation but does not give due consideration to the juridic elements involved might indeed be an invaluable source of information to one wishing to further his understanding of the role of the virtues, God's providence, His grace and man's cooperation with grace in the matter of religious vocation, and it can give rise to a valid and true *theological* concept of such a vocation. But the fact remains that a theological concept of religious vocation can be no more than just that, a theological concept; it is not the complete concept of vocation to the religious state as it exists today. For the state in question not only happens to have *de facto* existence as a juridic entity in the Church, (1) but, as shall be seen, in its present and precise form the

(1) The term "juridic" needs some explanation. Because all the various states of man equally fulfill the definition of the term state, it thence does not follow that all states alike

religious state is actually a product of the Church's own making, and acting in the fulness of the power given it by Christ, the Church reserves to itself the right to determine the necessary legal requirements for valid and licit entrance into it. Not to recognize the consequences of this fact in the matter of vocation is to close one's eyes to reality, and can result only in a distorted version of the complete and true concept.

Conversely a study which would so concentrate on the juridic aspect of religious vocation as to overlook or minimize the positiveness of God's role and His grace in the matter would give rise to no less an erroneous conclusion, despite whatever actual value such a study might have in contributing to an understanding of one or the other facet of the question. (2) It thus follows that the total concept of vocation to the religious state can be had only when the cognate theories of law and theology which go to form that concept are seen in proper relation one to the other, each receiving its due emphasis, each viewed in context, in the totality of which it forms a part, and *distinguer pour unir*, the indispensable precondition for all accurate thinking, must of necessity be the guiding norm of such a scientific juridical-theological approach.

Therefore, while the present study has as its immediate concern the Church's *legislation* relative to the question of religious vocation, and by means of a discerning examination seeks to derive what may be called a "juridic norm," the whole is to be viewed in the light of certain basic theological premises and conclusions, sometimes presumed, sometimes treated indirectly, sometimes given a more detailed, but by no means exhaustive, exposition. Such a procedure has a very evident advantage: while the necessary conclusions of theology are given their proper recognition and place in the total concept, and are seen even to contribute to and affect the crystallization of certain juridic elements, speculative theological controversies may be left in the speculative domain, so that they will not in the least engender any serious practical errors in the promoting of vocations, so long as the legislation is of such a tenor as to admit the possible proof of either side of the controversy. The fruit of such a work will be a practical guide which may be safely and confidently followed in determining the presence or absence of a religious vocation in a member of Christ's Mystical Body.

---

are juridical. For a state to be truly juridical it is necessary that the positive law should intervene, and so regulate determined facts that determined consequences (called juridical because they are the result of law) follow. The state of "nobility," for example, since it has no consideration of law, nor any special legal rights and obligations in most modern societies, cannot today be called a juridic state in those societies, although to give one example only, the "*plebs*" and the "*gens*" were recognized juridic states in Roman Law.

Some states today, however, do have recognition in law and are thus said to be juridically constituted; and from this juridical condition, which affects all the persons pertaining to them, there flow certain effects, rights and obligations which are sanctioned by the law itself, giving these states a character beyond that which they would possess without this added note. The state of marriage is an example. Marriage, as instituted by God, fulfills the definition of the term state, whether or no it would have any juridical recognition (beyond that, of course, which it has in God's own law). But once it has received this consideration of law, and has kept intact its fundamental essence, from a validly contracted and legal marriage follow all the juridic consequences foreseen by the legislator, both those which pertain to the couple itself and those which affect their children. Marriage then is no longer just a state; it is also a juridic state, and while it still possesses the essential elements it would have without this juridic consideration, the added elements of positive law give it a character beyond its fundamental nature, and place it within the province of the legislator. The legislator, of course, must have the power to act and also must confine his activity within the limits of his jurisdiction. This is fundamental. The Catholic Church, as a society by divine law distinct from the State and in its own order independent and supreme, as such has the power to legislate in that order for its own subjects. This is assumed in this study and is demonstrated in works of Dogmatic Theology. Cf. Goyeneche, "Studia Canonica," *Commentarium pro Religiosis* (Romae, 1920-; ab anno 1935: *Commentarium pro Religiosis et Missionariis*), I (1920), 25 (hereafter cited *CpR* or *CpRM*); Anonymous, "Studia Canonica," *CpRM*, XXV (1944-1946), 59.

(2) "Les Institutions de droit canonique enseignent les determinations positives que la dogmatique et la morale ont fait adopter."—Yelle, *Travail Scientifique en Disciplines Ecclésiastiques* (Montréal: Grand Séminaire de Montréal, 1945), p. 38.

Chapter II
THE MYSTICAL BODY AND VOCATION

Article I. The Mystical Body of Christ

The role of the religious in the Divine Economy cannot be adequately comprehended apart from the Doctrine of the Mystical Body of Christ, for again: a part cannot be understood out of its context, away from the totality from which it gets its meaning. Now the final end for which a religious has been created is identical with the final end of every other man who has existed: he is to be conformed to the image and likeness of Christ, (1) or, with a slightly different emphasis, his proper end consists in the supernatural love of God, (2) and according to the Divine Plan it is within the Mystical Body that this purpose is to be achieved. In the words of Pius XII:

> As he hung upon the Cross, Christ Jesus not only appeased the justice of the Eternal Father which had been violated, but He also won for us, His brethren, an ineffable flow of graces. It was possible for Him of Himself to impart these graces to mankind directly; but He willed to do so only through a visible Church made up of men, so that through her all might cooperate with Him in dispensing the graces of Redemption. As the Word of God willed to make use of our nature, when in excruciating agony He would redeem mankind, so in the same way throughout the centuries He makes use of the Church that the work begun might endure.
>
> If we would define and describe this true Church of Jesus Christ—which is the One, Holy, Catholic, Apostolic Roman Church—we shall find nothing more noble, more sublime, or more divine than the expression "the Mystical Body of Jesus Christ"—an expression which springs from and is, as it were, the fair flowering of the repeated teaching of the Sacred Scriptures and the holy Fathers. (3)

---

(1) "But 'if the Word emptied himself taking the form of a slave' (Philipp., II, 7), it was that He might make His brothers according to the flesh partakers of the divine nature (cf. II Peter, I, 4), through sanctifying grace in this earthly exile, in heaven through the joys of eternal bliss. For the reason why the only-begotten Son of the Eternal Father willed to be a son of man was that we might be made conformed to the image of the Son of God (cf. Rom., VIII, 29) and be renewed according to the image of Him who created us (cf. Col., III, 10)."—Pius XII, ep. encycl. *Mystici Corporis*, 29 iun. 1943—*Acta Apostolicae Sedis, Commentarium Officiale* (Romae, 1909-), XXXV (1943), 214 (hereafter cited as *AAS*). The translation of this encyclical used in this study is that printed by *Tipografia Polyglotta Vaticana* and published by the National Catholic Welfare Conference, Washington, D. C., the present citation being found in n. 46, p. 18.

(2) "Respondeo dicendum quod unumquodque dicitur esse perfectum, inquantum attingit proprium finem, qui est ultima rei perfectio. Caritas autem est quae unit nos Deo, qui est ultimus finis humanae mentis, quia 'qui manet in caritate, in Deo manet, et Deus in eo,' ut dicitur I Joan. 4, 16. Et ideo secundum caritatem specialiter attenditur perfectio christianae vitae."—St. Thomas (1225-1274), *Summa Theologica*, IIa, IIae, q. 184, a.1.

(3) Ep. encycl. *Mystici Corporis*—*AAS*, XXXV (1943), 198-199 (NCWC translation, nn. 12-13, pp. 7-8).

And the Head of this Body is Christ. (4)

This then is the reality of life in which the religious finds himself along with his fellow creatures, men bound into One Body, the Church, by the one life-stream flowing from the Head which is Christ. So St. Paul can say to the Romans, "We, the many, are one body in Christ"; (5) and to the Ephesians, "And all things he made subject under his feet, and him he gave as head over all the Church, which indeed is his body, the fullness of him who is wholly fulfilled in all"; (6) and to the Galatians, "For all you who have been baptized into Christ, have put on Christ. There is neither Jew nor Greek; there is neither slave nor freeman; there is neither male nor female. For you are all one in Christ Jesus." (7)

And it is particularly in his understanding of this doctrine of the Mystical Body that the religious comes to the full realization of the oft-repeated phrase "God loves variety." For the Mystical Body is not simply composed of a Head and an undifferentiated mass of human cells, all alike and all functioning alike. It is, like any other body, an organism, a structure, with different parts functioning differently for the perfection of the whole according to God's plan, the variety of human beings or cells corresponding to the variety of functions in that plan. Simply, God made men different from one another because they have different things to do, different functions to fill in an organic society. Again in the words of the present Holy Father:

> . . . as in nature a body is not formed by any haphazard grouping of members but must be constituted of organs, that is of members, that have not the same function and are arranged in due order; so for this reason above all the Church is called a body, that it is constituted by the coalescence of structurally united parts, and that it has a variety of members reciprocally dependent. It is thus the Apostle describes the Church when he writes: "As in one body we have many members, but all the members have not the same office: so we being many are one body in Christ, and every one members one of another. (Rom., XII, 4-5)."
>
> One must not think, however, that this ordered or "organic" structure of the body of the Church contains only hierarchical elements and with them is complete; . . . when the Fathers of the Church sing the praises of this Mystical Body of Christ, with its ministries, its variety of ranks, its offices, its conditions, its orders, its duties, they are thinking not only of those who have received Holy Orders, but of all those too, who, following the evangelical counsels, pass their lives either actively among men, or hidden in the silence of the cloister, or who aim at combining the active and contemplative life according to their Institute; as also of those who, though living in the world, consecrate themselves wholeheartedly to spiritual or corporal works or mercy, and of those who live in the state of holy matrimony. Indeed, let this be clearly understood, especially in these our days: fathers and mothers of families, those who are godparents through Baptism, and in particular those members of

(4) Cf. Col., I, 18.

(5) Rom. XII, 5. All direct quotations from the New Testament in this study are taken from the revision of the Challoner-Rheims Version by the Confraternity of Christian Doctrine (Paterson, N. J.: St. Anthony Guild Press, 1941).

(6) Ephesians, I, 22-23.

(7) Gal., III, 27-28.

the laity who collaborate with the ecclesiastical hierarchy in spreading the Kingdom of the Divine Redeemer occupy an honourable, if often lowly, place in the Christian community, and even they under the impulse of God and with His help, can reach the heights of supreme holiness, which Jesus Christ has promised, will never be wanting to the Church. (8)

In other words, pope and bishops and priests and religious and laymen must each become the image of Christ: so far there is no difference: there is not some greater likeness of Christ reserved to popes, some lesser likeness kept for the laity. But in the life processes of the Body, different members have different functions, which merely means that Christ uses them in different ways. This Body, like any other body, has an order and a proportion and a complexity of elements working together: some are eyes, some ears, some hands and some hearts, all different and all necessary, giving and getting life from the whole. In God's plan for His Body there is place for all: priest and religious, the married and the unmarried; the carpenter, the nurse, the poet; the young, the old, the strong and the weak: God makes no unnecessary people.

It is precisely the determining of God's plan in the concrete, in individual cases, "Where do I fit into God's plan? what is my functional place in the Mystical Body of Christ?" which brings up the question of vocation.

Article II. The Concept of Vocation: Its Nominal Definition

While "vocation" is a word which is commonly used today, it cannot be said that it is just as commonly understood. The ordinary person might use the term in a number of different senses and yet, according to popular usage, be correctly applying it in each instance. (9) The professions of law and medicine, for example, are often spoken of as "noble vocations," the word here being made synonymous with the professions themselves. In like manner the phrase "vocational guidance" is directly concerned with the various occupations for which an individual is best suited according to his abilities. (10) And very often,

(8) Pius XII, ep. encycl. *Mystici Corporis*, 29 iun. 1943—*AAS*, XXXV (1943), 200-201 (NCWC translation, nn. 16-17, pp. 8-9).

(9) Cf. *Webster's International Dictionary* (2. ed., Springfield: G. & C. Merriam Co., 1948), s.v. *vocation:* [L. *vocatio*, a bidding, a calling, invitation, fr. *vocare* to call; cf. F. *vocation*. See Vocal.] 1. A calling; a summons; a call; specif.: a. *Obs.* Convocation, as of an assembly. b. A calling to a particular state, business, or profession. 2. Regular or appropriate employment; calling; occupation; profession; as to change one's *vocation*. 3. The members of a particular calling or profession, collectively. *Rare.* 4. *Theol.* a. A calling to the service of God in a particular station or state of life, esp. in the priesthood or religious life, as shown by one's fitness, natural inclinations, and, often, by conviction of a Divine invitation. b. The station or state of life to which one receives such a calling. c. An official invitation to a particular ecclesiastical office, as a pastorate.

(10) In recent years much has been said and written about vocational guidance, and vocational counselors have assumed quite a place of prominence in our highly technological society. For the most part, however, and unfortunately so, the general plan of these "vocational experts" seems to be the redistribution of men and women to fit the existing economic and political systems without so much as a thought to God's will in the matter, either

as common experience shows, it is in the sense of an inclination, attraction or desire for a particular state of life, that the term is used.

Many Catholics, however, and not a few non-Catholics, when they speak of vocation are thinking of the term in its etymological meaning of a calling or summons, and in a more or less general and vague way they usually place the authority to issue that summons in the voice of God Himself calling the creature to some fixed responsibility and occupation, an interpretation that is in accord with the use of the word "called" (*vocatus*-κλητος) in the New Testament, which has always the sense of "called by God." (11) Catholics, moreover, when applying the word in this latter sense, according to a time-honored tradition, usually further restrict its meaning to "called by God to the priesthood or to the religious state," so much so, in fact, that when the article "a" precedes the word vocation without additional specification (e.g. "Has she or he a vocation?"), it is always understood that the reference is to a call by God to one or the other state. This too is commonplace and a fact of general experience.

In the present study the word vocation is always to be understood in its etymological sense: the action of summoning someone to move towards a definite goal. This already implies an authority to issue the call, and when that authority is understood to be God, then the vocation is called divine; when the authority issuing the summons is the Church, then the vocation is called ecclesiastical. Further specification of the vocation by such adjectives as "priestly" or "religious" merely designates the term towards which one is directed by the call. (12)

Vocation, therefore, is to be understood as an invitation or call to embrace a particular state or form of life: it is an action on the part of a superior directing a subject towards a goal; it is not the goal itself, but the necessary condition for its attainment. (13) Just what the exact nature of this call is when applied to the

---

as regards the individual *or* the system. There can be no denying the need for vocational guidance in the sense in which it is commonly used, but if such is to be truly fruitful for the individual, for the Church, and for society, it must be *Christian* vocational guidance, which takes into account the realities of the Mystical Body of Christ and the obligation of each member to lead an integral Christian life, not only in the Church but also in the world.

(11) Cf. Prat, *La Théologie de Saint Paul* (2 vols., Paris, 1908) I, 344.

(12) Vocation may also be looked upon in a passive as well as in an active sense. In its active modality, vocation is seen as the operation of an agent upon a subject calling him to a particular state; in its passive acceptation, vocation is viewed as the result produced in the subject who, *consequent upon the operation of the summoning agent*, has received the qualities demanded by the nature of that state. Vocation in this latter sense has particular reference to a divine calling and shall be considered in its proper place.

(13) This distinction between the call itself and the goal for which it is given is essential, for a confusion of these two separate entities can very well lead to false conclusions in the question of vocation. Olivero, for example, in contrasting vocation to the priesthood with vocation to the religious life, correctly points out that the subject of ordination is a passive subject upon whom the sacerdotal dignity is *conferred*, while the subject of religious profes-

religious state, whether it is divine, or ecclesiastical, or a combination of both; whether it is simply an external call, an internal call, or external *and* internal; addressed to all men, or only to a designated few, has been a problem much discussed in the Church for many centuries. This study seeks a practical answer in the legislation of the Church, always a safe guide to be confidently followed.

ARTICLE III. VOCATION IN THE MYSTICAL BODY

Because the concept of vocation traditionally has enjoyed a special application to the priesthood and to the religious state, and because this study limits its examination to matter which pertains to the latter state only, any consideration of vocation to another state being only for the purpose of shedding light on this primary objective in so far as it is or is not included in it, this is not to deny that the concept of vocation can legitimately have wider application and validly and profitably be used with reference to the other states of life in the Mystical Body. Indeed, to confine the notion of vocation to those who enter the priesthood or the religious life tends to establish a barrier between them and the rest of the faithful that is not at all intended by Christ, nor found in the teaching of the Scriptures and the tradition of the Church. Admittedly there is a gradation of places in the Mystical Body, those who have received Holy Orders and exercise sacred power in the Body being its first and chief members,

---

sion himself makes the act which is *received* by another, but from this truth he draws the conclusion that since, in contrast to ordination, nothing is *conferred* upon the religious subject at his profession, his admission into the religious state by a superior cannot properly be designated a vocation, but is merely a *conditio sine qua non* required by human law to perfect a vocation (divine) already given: "Praeterea maximum discrimen habetur quoad vocationem externam seu formalem, quae ex humano iure requiritur pro statu religioso, dum e contra pro statu clericali ex divino iure poscitur. Subiectus ordinationis *passive* se habet coram Episcopo qui illi sacerdotalem dignitatem confert, e contra religiosus in professione *active* se habet coram Superioribus qui eiusdem professionem recipiunt. Itaque admissio in religionem ex parte Superioris minus proprie vocatio nuncupatur, melius dici potest conditio sine qua non ad vocationem religionem perficiendam."—*De Vocatione Religiosa Clericorum Eorumque Facultate Religionem Ingrediendi* (Romae: Apud Custodiam Librariam Pont. Instituti Utriusque Iuris, 1947), p. 17 (hereafter cited *De Vocatione*).

The truth of the matter is that neither the act of ordination nor the act of religious profession is the vocation to those states, but they are rather the goals for which the particular calls are given. In priestly vocation the call itself is really distinct from, and a preparation for, the term of the vocation, namely sacerdotal ordination; in religious vocation, the call is likewise distinct from, and a preparation for, the term of vocation, namely the act of profession. The pointing out of this is not intended, even by way of anticipation, as an argument one way or the other concerning the nature of religious vocation, nor as a dismissal, as something inconsequential, of the truth contained in the passage cited; it is intended simply to show the necessity of making a real distinction between the vocation and its goal, if premature conclusions are to be avoided. For a further treatment of the distinction between the call and its term cf. Farrell, *The Theology of Religious Vocation* (St. Louis: B. Herder, 1951) pp. 40-43 (hereafter cited *Theology of Religious Vocation*).

(14) but mindful with Saint Paul that "the eye cannot say to the hand, 'I do not need thy help'; nor again the head to the feet, 'I have no need of you.' Nay, much rather, those that seem the more feeble members of the body are more necessary. . . . " (15) this study in excluding any particular consideration of vocation to the married state, for example, or to the single life in the world, does not mean to relegate these members to a "second-class citizenship" in the Kingdom of Heaven or make them feel like stepchildren in the house of their Father. Since, as has been pointed out, the perfection of the Mystical Body as a whole is attained only by the carrying out of a myriad of proper functions by the individual members of the Body who, in the successful accomplishment of their specific tasks, at the same time bring about that perfection and their own salvation, others besides those who are considering the priesthood or the religious life can logically look to God, acting personally or through the ministry of His chosen ambassadors, (16) for indications of His will as to their proper place in this organic society, and they may legitimately inquire about their vocation or call to it. (17) These particular vocations may be expressed internally, through the promptings of grace, or externally indicated more or less clearly to each man by his abilities, inclinations, opportunities, and a thousand other signs which God makes use of, but a precise examination of the exact nature of these vocations the writer leaves to others. It is when the question is phrased "Is my functional role in the Mystical Body that of being a religious? Have I a religious vocation?" that the proper subject of this study is brought into focus.

The remainder of this dissertation looks to the great body of Church legislation, both in its present form and in its historical development, for a practical guide in answering this specific question. To repeat the fundamental position taken in the first chapter of this section, while the norm derived might correctly be called juridic, full recognition is given to the fact that, since the role of the

(14) Pius XII, ep. encycl. *Mystici Corporis*, 29 iun. 1943—*AAS*, XXXV (1943), 200 (NCWC translation, n. 17, p. 9).

(15) I Cor., XII, 20-22.

(16) "To the members He (Christ) is present and assists them in proportion to their various duties and offices and the greater or less degree of spiritual health which they enjoy. It is He who through His heavenly grace is the principle of every supernatural act in all parts of the Body. It is He who while He is personally present and divinely active in all the members, nevertheless in the inferior members acts also through the ministry of the higher members."—Pius XII, *op. cit.*, *AAS*, XXXV (1943), 219-220 (NCWC translation, n. 57, p. 22).

(17) Cf., for example, what Pius XII has to say concerning the vocations of those individuals who, while remaining in the world (that is, who are not members of any religious order or congregation), strive in a special way for perfection in the Consociations known as "Secular Institutes": const. *Provida Mater Ecclesia*, 2 febr. 1947—*AAS*, XXXIX (1947), 117; 118; motu propr. *De Institututorum Saecularium Laude atque Confirmatione*, 12 mart. 1948—*AAS*, XL (1948), 283; 286.

religious in the Mystical Body must essentially exist for and be subordinate to the supernatural end of the entire Body, the restoration of all things in Christ, the role of Divine Providence, grace and free will necessarily enters into any complete concept of religious vocation, and these theological realities must be given due consideration. But it must also be established as fundamental that the necessary conclusions of theology are to be employed in this study only in the measure in which they are recognized by the law itself and serve to illuminate and explain it, for this study is to be above all a practical study, and therefore must leave detailed discussion of the theoretical problems of theology to theologians.

PART II
Vocation to the Juridic Religious State

Chapter III
THE NATURE OE THE JURIDIC RELIGIOUS STATE

Since the nature of a thing is ultimately determined by its final object, that is, the purpose or end for which it exists, (1) it is obvious that, unless one fully understands that object or purpose, one's knowledge of the thing itself will be incomplete, and like as not constitute a half-truth that, as often happens, is no truth at all. Now, as has been stated and is patently evident, it is the function of a religious vocation to lead an individual to embrace the religious state; it logically terminates in that object. Therefore, an examination of the nature of the religious state itself is in order before consideration can be given to vocation to that state, for the religious state is the goal towards which one is directed by the call; it is the end which gives form to the means. The present chapter purposes to make such an examination by considering the religious state first in its primordial sense, that is, as essentially established by Christ, and then in its present developed state, as it exists today, with the elements given it by Our Lord crystallized and substantially added to by the Church. This procedure appears desirable not only because it happens to conform to the chronological order of things, but also because it is a perfectly logical process to inspect the parts which go to make up the whole, before the whole is viewed in its entirety. Moreover, such a method will by anticipation help to emphasize the fact that, inasmuch as the religious state as established by Christ and the religious state as it juridically exists today are not substantially coextensive, the notion of vocation for the one might very well be inadequate for the other. The distinction is important, therefore, and is an application of the principle "*distinguer pour unir.*"

Article I. The Primordial Religious State: Its Origin and Nature

Man, it has been pointed out, is to be conformed to the image and likeness of Christ, a goal to be achieved through the exercise of love—love of God and,

(1) Cf. Meyer-Eckhoff, *The Philosophy of St. Thomas Aquinas* (St. Louis: Herder, 1948), p. 69.

in Him and for Him, love of neighbor: therein lies man's perfection; therein lies the very purpose for his existence. (2) Such was the burden of Our Lord's three years' public ministry to mankind which had worked out all the bleak logic of self-assertion and discovered for itself all the unwholesome places into which self-assertion could take it. By word and example He taught the love of God: in no other way can man attain his proper end; no activity not subordinated to it can have legitimate existence.

Everyone without exception, therefore, must love God, and in its minimum degree that love consists in the faithful observance of the commandments. "Good master, what good work shall I do to have eternal life?" has for its answer, "If thou wilt enter into life, keep the commandments." (3) This is the essential minimum incumbent upon all men; it is also the lowest degree of perfection.

But because to aim for the minimum of perfection in this matter, which is the most important of all man's concerns, is neither a generous expression of filial love and gratitude, nor, at least in most cases, even a safe design, and because He realized that not all men, once they had come to know God, could be satisfied with the bare necessities of love, Our Lord voiced His ultimate challenge to man, "You therefore are to be perfect, even as your Heavenly Father is perfect," (4) and assured him of the further means open to all who desire to advance on the road to perfection: "If thou wilt be perfect . . . come follow me." (5) Christ's life and His teaching is replete with examples of how man may thus strive to ever higher degrees of perfection and progress in His love of God: the practice of perfect chastity, of poverty, of obedience; the love and care of the sick, the poor, the downtrodden—these are but a few of His suggestions to all men of good will who would love God more and in so doing become more perfect. And it is precisely in His teaching of these evangelical counsels that Christ is regarded as the founder of the religious state in its fundamental nature and essence. (6)

(2) Cf. *supra*, p. 4.

(3) St. Matthew, XIX, 16-17; cf. also St. John, XIV, 15: "If you love me, keep my commandments."

(4) St. Matthew, V, 48

(5) St. Matthew, XIX, 21.

(6) This doctrine, that Our Lord is the immediate founder of the religious state as regards its substantial elements, is the common teaching of the Fathers and Doctors of the Church and is profusely treated by them. It is difficult to see how the opposite opinion, that the religious state is *merely* an ecclesiastical institution, can be held without temerity. Cf. Suarez (1548-1617), *De Religione*, *Opera Omnia* (26 vols. in 28, editio nova a Carolo Berton, Parisiis: apud Ludovicum Vivès, 1856-1868), tr. 7, lib. 3, c. 2, nn. 3, 4, 5; Vol. XV, pp. 231-232; Muzzarelli, *De Professione Religiosa a Primordiis ad Saeculum XII* (Romae: Apud Piam Societatem Sancti Pauli, 1938), pp. 15-19 (hereafter cited Muzzarelli); Bouix, *Tractatus de Jure Regularium* (2 vols., Parisiis, 1857), I, 129 (hereafter cited *De Jure Regularium*); Prümmer, *Manuale Iuris Canonici* (3. ed., Friburgi Brisgoviae: Herder & Co., 1922), p. 238 (here-

In itself, therefore, and in abstraction from any notion of that state as a juridic institute in the Church, the religious life is nothing more than a private state in which Christians embrace the evangelical counsels in an enduring manner, an activity mediately and immediately ordained to the attainment of that perfection which consists in the love of God in a degree beyond the absolute minimum required. (7) Essential to this concept, the very *raison d'etre* of the religious life, is the pursuance of higher perfection, the *finis sanctificationis,* (8) and this through the observance of the evangelical counsels. (9) But while it is true that the observance of even one of the evangelical counsels in an enduring manner (e.g. chastity) would fundamentally constitute one in the religious state, nevertheless in its complete and strict sense, even fundamentally, there must be included the observance of all the three principal counsels, namely, poverty,

---

after cited *Manuale*); Wernz-Vidal, *Ius Canonicum ad Codicis Normam Exactum* (7 tomes in 8 vols., Tom. III, *De Religiosis*, Romae: apud Aedes Universitatis Gregorianae, 1933), III, 29-30, n. 28 (hereafter cited *De Religiosis*); Molitor, *Religiosi Iuris Capita Selecta* (Ratisbonae, 1909), p. 2 (hereafter cited Molitor). This is not to say that Christ Himself immediately established various religious institutes with their special and particular end and their proper accidental forms, although Suarez is of the opinion that Our Lord did establish such a particular religious institute and received the Apostles into it with the profession of vows (*De Religione*, tr. 7, lib. 3, c. 2, n. 9; Vol. XV, p. 233). But this opinion, while possible and not lacking a certain intrinsic probability, cannot be demonstrated by any direct and historical arguments. Cf. Schaefer, *De Religiosis ad Normam Codicis Iuris Canonici* (4. ed., Roma: Typis Polyglottis Vaticanis, 1947), p. 17 (hereafter cited *De Religiosis*); Wernz-Vidal, *De Religiosis*, p. 29, note (3).

(7) This study is concerned with the religious *state*, and therefore makes no attempt to consider the rôle of the evangelical counsels in the lives of those who only intermittently pursue a higher degree of perfection than the minimum required. The term *state* etymologically derives from the word *stare*, to stand, and metaphorically designates a manner of existing or living which has a certain similitude with a man who is standing, that is, one who is immobile. In its strict sense, therefore, *state* connotes a fixed manner of living, regularly permanent and not easily mutable. Cf. *Summa Theologica*, IIa, IIae, q. 183, a. 1; Suarez, *De Religione*, tr. 7, lib. 1, c. 1, nn. 1, 2, 3, 9; Vol. XV, pp. 2-3, 4-5. With reference to the religious life, the term *state* denotes a fixed manner of living which has perfection for its object, and the evangelical counsels for its means.

(8) "If thou wilt be perfect . . . come, follow me,"—St. Matthew, XIX, 21; "Scopus istius status praecise in eo consistir, quod quis stabiliter et perseverenter tendat ad perfectionem."—Bachofen, *Compendium Juris Regularium* (Neo Eboraci, 1903), p. 10 (hereafter cited *Compendium*); cf. *Normae*, June 28, 1901, where the *finis sanctificationis* is called the primary, the general, the proper, the substantial end of the religious life (quoted in Schaefer, *De Religiosis*, pp. 1102-1136); cf. also Wernz-Vidal, *De Religiosis*, pp. 4-6, nn. 5-6; *Summa Theologica*, IIa, IIae, q. 184, a. 2, 5; q. 186, a. 1; Suarez, *De Religione*, tr. 7, lib. 2, c. 1, n. 2; Vol. XV, p. 114.

(9) *Summa Theologica*, IIa, IIae, q. 184, a. 3; cf. also Schaefer, *De Religiosis*, pp. 13-16; Muzzarelli, pp. 16-19, where these authors prove at great length that Our Lord by His example and doctrine established these primary means of striving for perfection.

chastity, and obedience. (10) For these three, as Saint Thomas pointed out, are both necessary and sufficient to remove all the impediments which stand in the way of man's whole-hearted love of God, being directed as they are against the threefold concupiscence of which Saint John speaks:

If anyone loves the world, the love of the Father is not in him; because all that is in the world is the lust of the flesh, and the lust of the eyes, and the pride of life. (11)

Wherefore, poverty which militates against the allurements of the world with its riches and comforts, chastity which strives against the flesh and its unruly passions and its desire for pleasure, obedience which pits itself against self-love, ever proud, ever striving to gain the mastery over others, are the three means, required and sufficient, that the religious state (at least abstractly considered) might be complete, and that man might give himself totally to the pursuit of that perfection which consists in the greatest love of which a human creature is capable inasmuch as he has removed from himself every impediment to such a love, offering himself a "holocaust to God." (12) But while it has also long been the general opinion of authors that the pursuit of perfection through the

(10) This distinction between the religious state in its strict sense and in its general sense is a mere assertion of fact and is the unanimous usage among authors. Cf. Suarez, *De Religione;* tr. 7, lib. 2, c. 1, n. 1; Vol. XV, p. 113: "Principio supponendum est, iuxta communem Ecclesiae usum, statum religiosum, quasi per antonomasim, et stricta significatione, appellari perfectum monachorum seu regularium statum, qui se Deo totaliter consecrant et tradunt, tria vota de tribus principalibus consiliis, paupertatis, castitatis et obedientiae, emittendo. Nihilominus tamen latiori seu generaliori quodam significato, status religionis sub se comprehendit alios vivendi modos, in quibus homines voluntarie se offerunt divino cultui et obsequio, ad aliquam consiliorum observationem se obligando. Et sic comprehendit non tantum proprios et completos religiosos, sed etiam continentes, qui per solum votum castitatis se Deo specialiter obligant; vel quoscumque alios, qui non integre, sed ex parte vota religiosorum emittunt. Sic enim juris canonici interpretes in Rubr. de Regul. docent, nomen religiosi vel regularis, stricte sumptum, significare eum, qui tria substantialia vota comprehendere omnes, qui per aliquod votum et specialem vivendi modum Dei servitio consecrantur." Cf. also Schmalzgrueber, *Ius Ecclesiasticum Universum* (5 vols. in 12, Romae, 1843-1845), lib. 3, tit. 31, nn. 1, 2 (hereafter cited *Ius Ecclesiasticum*). To be a religious in the strict sense one must strive after perfection by taking the means to remove *all* the obstacles which hinder union with God. Cf. Bouix, *De Jure Regularium*, I, 37.

(11) I John, II, 15-16.

(12) Cf. *Summa Theologica*, IIa, IIae, q. 186, a. 7, where Saint Thomas shows how all the obstacles which proceed from the threefold concupiscence and impede the acquiring of perfection are overcome by these three vows. Cf. also Suarez, *De Religione*, tr. 7, lib. 2, c. 2, nn. 10-16; Vol. XV, pp. 120-122; Vermeersch, "De status religiosi essentia et interpretatione can. 487 et 488", *Periodica de Re Canonica et Morali utilia praesertim Religiosis et Missionariis* (Brugis, 1905-), XV (1926-1927), (5) (hereafter cited *Periodica*). Pius XI in his apostolic letter *Unigenitus*, March 19, 1924, described the value of the evangelical counsels in these words: "Eiusmodi autem consilia quicumque, obligata Deo fide, servaturum se spondeat, is non modo omnibus exsolvitur impedimentis quae mortales a sanctitate remorari solent, ut bona fortunae, ut coniugii curae sollicitudinesque, ut immoderata rerum omnium libertas; sed etiam tam recto expeditoque itinere ad perfectionem vitae progreditur, ut iamiam in salutis portu anchoram velut iecisse videatur."—*AAS*, XVI (1924), 133.

observance of the evangelical counsels can *de facto* be rendered firm only through the taking of the three *vows* of poverty, chastity and obedience, (13) vows do not seem to be required precisely from the nature of the religious state itself; for the required stability which the religious state demands can inherently be achieved by other means, e.g., by the taking of an oath, (14) and besides, Christ made no mention of vows when exhorting to the observance of the evangelical counsels. (15)

Moreover, the essential character of the religious state does not require that it possess a social (as opposed to individual) nature. In other words, while that activity of love which finds expression in working with, and particularly for, one's neighbor is a natural concomitant of man's love of God, (16) the common life (17) does not pertain to the essence of the religious state as established by Christ: one need not be incorporated into any religious society to be a religious in the strict sense of the word. (18) Anchorites, therefore, are true religious in the sense that the term has been accepted in this article, and although, as shall be seen, long-standing discipline has required the observance of the common life for the *juridic* religious state, so that the strictly eremitical life no longer pertains to *that* state, such a form of life is not prohibited by the Church even today, (19) and moreover is not only accepted by the Oriental Discipline also, but is even compatible with the juridically recognized religious state of that Discipline. (20)

---

(13) *Summa Theologica*, IIa, IIae, q. 186, a. 6; Suarez, *De Religione*, tr. 7, lib. 2, c. 4, n. 5; Vol. XV, pp. 128-129; Bouix, *De Jure Regularium*, I, 44; Schaefer, *De Religiosis*, p. 53. No other cause seems sufficient to these authors to guarantee the stability required by the religious state.

(14) Coronata, *Institutiones Iuris Canonici ad Usum Utriusque Cleri et Scholarum* (5 vols., Vol. I, 2. ed., Taurini, Romae: Marietti, 1939), I, 605 (hereafter cited *Institutiones*); Larraona, "*Commentarium Codicis*," *CpR*, II (1921), 170.

(15) "Dictum est . . . vota in professione requiri de jure communi. Non autem dicitur de jure divino, quia nec de Evangelio nec de traditione, nec de lege naturae aliquid hujusmodi duci potest."—Molitor, p. 7.

(16) Cf. I John, IV, 20-21.

(17) The nature of the "common life" and all that the term implies shall be considered in the article immediately following. For the present it is sufficient to define it with reference to the religious life as the pursuit of perfection within the confines and membership of an organized group.

(18) "Sine vita communi potest status verus religionis constitui."—Suarez, *De Religione*, tr. 7, lib. 2, c. 4, n. 4; Vol. XV, p. 128 cf. also Schmalzgrueber, *Ius Ecclesiasticum*, lib. 3, tit. 31, n. 20, where he contrasts the religious state as considered in itself with the religious state as a juridical institute, with regard to the question of the common life.

(19) Cf. Wernz, *Ius Decretalium* (2. ed., 6 vols., Romae et Prati, 1905-1914), III, n. 590, III (hereafter cited *Ius Decretalium*); Wernz-Vidal, *De Religiosis*, p. 9, n. 8, III.

(20) Cf. Coussa, *Epitome Praelectionum de Iure Ecclesiastico Orientali* (2 vols., Vol. II, Venetiis: Typis Polyglottis Insulae S. Lazari, 1941), II, 11-13 (hereafter cited *Epitome*). Any solitary form of life, however, must be lived in accordance with the reality of life in the

Finally, the private pursuit of perfection through the observance of the three vows, inherently or from the nature of the matter does not need the positive approbation of the Church, in order that it exist as the true religious state. (21) That which can be present or absent without intrinsically changing a thing does not pertain to the substance of that thing, and the religious state as established by Christ intrinsically remains the same with or without ecclesiastical approbation. For the observance of the three vows of poverty, chastity and obedience is what intrinsically constitutes that state, and the approbation of the Church is merely an act of ecclesiastical superiors declaring that form of life to be good, patently an extrinsic act, since the mere declaration of goodness neither constitutes a thing good nor intrinsically changes the nature of its goodness. (22)

This then, in brief, is the religious state as essentially constituted by Christ: it is a private, individual state, in which man not merely strives for goodness, but also aspires to perfection; in which he accepts not only the precepts of the gospel, but its advice also: marriage, property, personal will, by a generous effort of his free choice he lays upon the altar of sacrifice, and thus stripped of self he offers to God a complete and perfect holocaust. Viewed in the light of the Mystical Body, it is easy to see how closely the end of this state approxi-

---

Mystical Body. Sheed expresses this point very well when, speaking of the nature and necessity of prayer, he says: "Because man is not an isolated unit, each man related only to God and no man to any other, but all related to God and therefore to one another, there must be a social element in prayer as well as an individual. Men go apart to pray, for each has his own incommunicable self which is only his; but they must come together to pray too. This again would be true in any event, given that men exist in the solidarity of the human race. But it reaches a new depth in the unity of the Mystical Body. There is a prayer of the whole Body, a prayer which Christ as Head of the Body makes His own and offers as His own; and it would be an appalling impoverishment of our life in the Body to take no conscious willed part of it. The Christian's private prayer, the conversation of himself *as himself* with God is essential, though even in this the Christian remains *in* the Body and prays from his place in the Body; but liturgical prayer, the prayer of the Body itself, is essential too. God loves both, and the Christian grows by both."—*Theology and Sanity* (New York: Sheed and Ward, 1946), p. 284.

(21) Bouix, *De Jure Regularium*, I, 56-64; Wernz-Vidal, *De Religiosis*, p. 11.

(22) *Negative* approbation of the Church is presumed, for a state of perfection which has been prohibited or declared invalid by the Church is a manifest contradiction. Moreover, let it be observed that by the very nature of things and in virtue of his divine commission to guide the faithful not only in the way of the precepts, but also in the path of the counsels (cf. St. John, XXI, 15-17), direction of the generous souls who have embraced the state of perfection is entrusted to the Roman Pontiff, who can, therefore, keeping intact its fundamental nature, prescribe by general and particular laws whatever is necessary or useful for the conservation and development of that life, a similar prerogative being possessed by the bishops throughout the world, acting individually or together in assembly, but always in union with and under the supreme authority of the Holy See (cf. St. Matthew, XXVIII, 18-20). But since the religious life is only of counsel and obligatory only in virtue of and according to the terms of the individual's pact with God, papal and episcopal authority is limited to the obligation assumed through the particular "religious profession."

mates the end of the Christian life in general. (23) For with the religious it is not only a question of subordinating his particular activity in the Body to the ultimate and all-embracing goal of perfection; he actually makes that general goal his *special* work in the organism, so that while others sanctify themselves through the perfect fulfillment of a myriad specific functions, the religious concentrates directly on the pursuit of sanctity itself by going beyond the mere demands of justice, of nature, even of the divine precept of love, and dedicates to God all that he is and all that he has. He not only strives after perfection, as indeed all men must; he is, so to speak, a professional perfectionist.

Personal sanctification, then, is the major and all-consuming interest in the life of the individual who has embraced the religious state as established by Christ, (24) but by no means should it be interpreted as inordinate self-interest. To do so would be to miss the entire point of the life he has espoused, for the religious has accepted the way of the counsels with the immediate purpose of his own perfection in mind precisely and ultimately for the greater honor and glory of God, and this as an augmentation of the "greatest and first commandment." (25) One who is self-minded in this sense is God-minded. Likewise the social aspects of even a strictly eremitical life are not to be overlooked. For just as those, for example, who give themselves to the duty of procreation are seeing to the welfare of the Mystical Body from the material point of view, so also those who give themselves up to the life of the counsels are seeing to the welfare of the same Body from the spiritual point of view. (26) No body is stronger than its weakest cell, and therefore every supernaturally strong and healthy member of the Mystical Body by the very fact of his own personal well-being contributes to the health and well-being of the entire organism. One may here accommodate the words of Robert Gordon Anderson who, remarkably, was writing as a non-Catholic at the time:

> Whenever one through sacrifice and complete surrender to the inflowing currents of God's love, becomes truly a saint, not only do those in Heaven rejoice quite as they do over the finding of the parable's lost sheep, but the whole Church, the whole body of believers everywhere, is given strength, enriched. There is a heartening and beautiful principle of the higher life which every creed accepts that speaks of the Communion of Saints. And all of

(23) Cf. *Summa Theologica*, Ia, IIae, q. 58, a. 4: "Oportet igitur quod praecepta novae legis intelligantur esse data de his quae sunt necessaria ad consequendum finem aeternae beatitudinis, in quem lex nova immediate introducit; consilia vero oportet esse de illis per quae melius et expeditius potest homo consequi finem praedictum."

(24) For purposes of contrast it should be noted that Christ established the *priesthood* essentially for the sanctification of others (*sacerdos propter alios*), and only secondarily for the sanctification of the one possessing the sacerdotal character. Cf. Carr, *Vocation to the Priesthood: Its Canonical Concept*, The Catholic University of America Canon Law Studies, n. 293 (Washington, D. C.: The Catholic University of America Press, 1950), pp. 13, 16 (hereafter cited *Vocation to the Priesthood*).

(25) Cf. St. Matthew, XXII, 35-37.

(26) Cf. Messenger, *Two in One Flesh* (3 vols., London: Sands & Co., 1948), III, 14.

the higher vision know with that knowledge and certainty that is born of faith and experience that this law, mystical yet in its results so practical, works in this way: By every increment of such holy and sweet lives the power of the Church is increased; and there is an enrichment of a vast treasury and reserve of the spirit which helps all believers, even though they are unaware of it, and on which every soul can draw for sustenance and comfort. (27)

And this is perfectly in accord with the mind of Saint Thomas:

. . . it is necessary to the multitude not only that it should be multiplied bodily, but also that it should progress spiritually. And hence the multitude will be provided for sufficiently if some give themselves to the work of carnal generation, and others, abstaining from this, give themselves to the contemplation of divine things, for the glory and well-being of the whole human race. (28)

. . . for the perfection of the human community, it is necessary that some should devote themselves to the contemplative life. (29)

The religious life in this its primordial sense, therefore, is of practical concern to all. Academically, however, it is more the concern of the theologian than the province of the canonist.

Article II. The Juridic Religious State: Its Origin and Nature

1. The origin of the juridic religious state, its development and crystallization

The religious state remained primarily the concern of the theologian for some years. For while the Acts of the Apostles (30) and particularly the writings of the early Fathers (31) bear witness that, from the very beginning of Christianity,

(27) *The Biography of a Cathedral* (New York: Longmans, Green and Co., 1946), pp. 322-323. Also apropos is his observation in the preceding paragraph: "In the fields of radioactivity, thermodynamics, all those of physics, there are infinitely fine instruments for the gauging of energy. . . . But there is no precision instrument for measuring the galvanic power of prayer which despite the wistful scoffing of purblind pragmatic skeptics, has been proven time and time again by lofty and consecrated souls to be limitless and as potent and as positive as only the truly ideal can be. And very early the monks, particularly those of the more purely contemplative orders, projected their prayers, if not their practical service, out from their cells, over their walls, to the remotest corners of the world. They prayed not only for themselves but for all sorts and conditions of men, for their enlightenment and salvation and their acceptance of the love of God. This had always been one of the noblest purposes of the most consecrated orders."—*op. cit.*, p. 322.

(28) *Summa Theologica*, IIa, IIae, q. 152, a. 2.

(29) *Op. cit.*, Pars III, Suppl., q. 41, a. 2.

(30) Cf. Acts II, 44-45; IV, 32-36; XXI, 9; cf. also St. Paul, I Cor. VII, 1ff.

(31) Cf. St. Ignatius (d.c. 110), *Ad Polycarpum*, c. 5 (Migne, *Patrologiae Cursus Completus Series Graeca*, 161 vols., Parisiis, 1857-1866, V, 723 (hereafter cited *MPG*); St. Clement of Rome, (d.c. 97), *Epistola I ad Corinth.*, c. 38 (*MPG*, I, 283); Hermas b.?-d.?), lib. III, *similitudo* IX, c. 29 (*MPG*, II, 1003); St. Polycarp (d.c. 155), *Ad Philippen. V* (*MPG*, V, 1009); St. Justin (d.c. 165), *Apologia I pro Christianis* (*MPG*, VI, 965); Clement of Alexandria (c. 150-c. 215), *Stromata*, lib. III, c. 1, 15 (*MPG*, VIII, 1098-1198); *Paedagogus*, lib. II, c. 2 (*MPG*, VIII, 378-442); Hippolytus (fl. 2. cent.), *Fragmenta In Proverb.* (*MPG*, X, 627); *De Virgine Corinthica* (*MPG*, X, 871-874); Origen (c. 185-254), *Hom. 2* (*MPG*, XII, 590); *In Matth., hom. 15* (*MPG*, XIII, 1295); Eusebius, *Hist. Eccl.* lib. VI, c. 3 (*MPG*, XX, 530); Tertullian (d. after 220), *Ad uxorem*, lib. I, c. 7-8 (Migne, *Patrologiae Cursus Completus Series Latina*, 221

individuals of both sexes, inspired by the teaching and example of their Master, responded generously to the Gospel counsels and engaged in the pursuit of evangelical perfection, and while, therefore, the practice of the religious life may without exaggeration be traced back in an unbroken line to the time of the Apostles themselves, (32) the first three centuries saw this life retain its primordial nature of a personal affair and private state. It is true that from the very first the Church in its *magisterium* admitted and recognized the pursuit of evangelical perfection, wisely sanctioning and strongly defending it, and at the same time developed the doctrine and example of Christ by securely teaching how a life devoted to perfection was to be lived and properly ordered, (33) but there are no indications of the Church's having taken the initiative or having placed all these souls under its special charge, nor is there to be found anywhere in ecclesiastical legislation a canonical recognition of the life of perfection. In the first and second centuries the ascetics and the virgins were distinguished from the rest of the faithful mainly by their perfect continence, (34) by which par-

vols., Parisiis, 1844-1855, I, 1286-1287 (hereafter cited *MPL*); *De resurrectione carnis*, c. 8 (*MPL*, II, 806); *De virginibus velandis* (*MPL*, II, 887-914); St. Cyprian (d. 258), *Epistola LXII* (*MPL*, IV, 365-372); *Testimon. adv. Judaeos*, lib. III, c. 74 (*MPL*, IV, 771); *De habitu virginum* (*MPL*, IV, 439-464). This listing, while by no means exhaustive, is indicative of the patristic doctrine.

(32) Most authors, however, because of an apparent reluctance to apply the term "religious" except in its complete and strict sense (cf. *supra*, p. 14, note 10), do not generally concede that the persons spoken of in the Acts were members of the religious state in its essential elements, and would consider them rather as leading a life which only to a degree partook of the nature of the religious life. Some authors, however, see here the religious state properly so called. Cf. Salmeron, (1515-1585) *Commentaria in Acta Apostolorum*, tom. XII, tr. XIX, pp. 120-121, the passage being quoted in full in Muzzarelli, pp. 28-29; cf. also Bouix, *De Jure Regularium*, I, 146-161.

In like manner, while most modern historians of the religious life usually begin with an account of the lives of the men and women of the early Church who were extolled in the writing of the Fathers as the "ascetics" and "virgins", they also hesitate to designate them as religious in the strict sense of the term, their hesitancy again stemming from the fact that there is not sufficient historical evidence at hand to prove that they bound themselves by the profession of the *three* vows which go to make up the *complete religious state*. Cf. Schaefer *De Religiosis*, p. 20; Wernz, *Ius Decretalium*, III, n. 590. Schaefer, however, does admit that there are vestiges of the free renunciation of temporal goods and of perfect obedience; and some authors, e.g. Muzzarelli, p. 53, see in these vestiges enough to warrant saying that the essential elements of the religious state required by its very nature were present, and that religious in the strict sense did therefore exist from the very first century.

(33) Pius XII, const. *Provida Mater Ecclesia*, 2 febr. 1947—*AAS*, XXXIX (1947), 114.

(34) It cannot be demonstrated with any degree of historical certitude, however, that the virgins and ascetics of the first two centuries bound themselves by a vow, at least expressed, to persevere in the way of life they had chosen. It is certain that they did so in the following century (cf. Clement of Alexandria, *Stromata*, III (*MPG*, VIII, 1103, 1198); Origen, *Hom. in Levit.*, n. 196 (*MPG*, XII, 428); cf. also Tertullian, *De velandis virginibus*, c. 6 (*MPL*, II, 911); St. Cyprian, *De hab. virg.*, c. 4 (*MPL*, IV, 443-444), although no public ceremony

ticularly they were considered to reflect honor on the Christian name, (35) but to which they also added other works and mortifications. (36) Even in the third century (37) when they were beginning to constitute in the bosom of the Church a distinct order and social class, (38) forming a sort of spiritual aristocracy and receiving marks of peculiar respect, (39) the virgins and the ascetics did not enjoy any distinct juridical status beyond that which they possessed as members of the clergy or the laity, (40) for which reason, therefore, one cannot

or solemnity was associated with the taking of the vow until the middle of the fourth century when, at least among the virgins, a change of garb and the investiture with the veil became recognized as specific signs of the act of profession. Cf. St. Ambrose (333/340-397), *De Virginibus*, III, c. 1 (*MPL*, XVI, 219); *Canones Synodi Romani* (c. 400), c. 1—Mansi, *Sacrorum Conciliorum Nova et Amplissima Collectio* (53 vols. in 59, Parisiis, Arnhemii, Lipsiae, 1901-1927), III, 1134 (hereafter cited Mansi).

(35) Cf. Athenagoras, *Legatio pro Christianis*—*MPG*, VI, 966; St. Justin, *I Apolog.* c. 15—*MPG*, VI, 350; St. Clement of Rome, *I Ep. ad Corinth.*—*MPG*, I, 283; St. Ignatius, *Ep. ad Polycarpum*—*MPG*, V, 723.

(36) Prayer and self-denial, along with fast and abstinence were part of their daily lives, and there were not lacking indications of perfect obedience among them, although early history has little to say concerning this phase of their life. Cf. Wernz, *Ius Decretalium*, III, 630, n. 601.

(37) Historical testimony of the period gives evidence that by this time many of the virgins and ascetics voluntarily disposed of their property and conformed their lives to the evangelical counsel of poverty. Cf. St. Cyprian, *De hab. virg.* (*MPL*, IV, 448-449); St. Ambrose, *De Virg.* I, c. 2 (*MPL*, XVI, 206); St. Gregory Nazianzus (329/330-c. 390), *De Vita S. Greg. Thau.* (*MPG*, XLVI, 907); Eusebius, *Hist. Eccl.*, VI, 3 (*MPG*, XX, 530); *De vita et passione S. Cypriani*, c. 2 (*MPL*, III, 1484).

(38) Pius XII, const. *Provida Mater Ecclesia*, 2 febr. 1947—*AAS*, XXXIX (1947), 114.

(39) Clement of Alexandria called them "the elect among the elect."—*Quis dives salv.*, c. 36 (*MPG*, IX, 642); St. Cyprian spoke of the virgins in these beautiful words: " . . . ecclesiastici germinis flores, decus et ornamentum gratiae spiritualis laeta indoles, laudis et honoris opus integrum atque incorruptum, Dei imago respondens ad sanctimonium Domini illustriorem portionem gregis Christi."—*De hab. virg.* (*MPL*, IV, 445); Origen placed them after the deacons when enumerating the diverse states in the Church (cf. *In Num. hom.* 2, c. 1—*MPG*, XII, 591), and St. Hippolytus numbered the ascetics fifth among the seven divine orders—*Fragmenta in Proverbia* (*MPG*, X, 627). Although they had not yet assumed a distinctive garb, they were expected always to be recognizable for what they were, and this not only by their life of chastity and ascèticism, but even by their modest dress and lack of finery: "Virgo non esse tantum sed et intelligi debet et credi. Nemo cum virginem viderit, dubitet an virgo sit."—St. Cyprian, *De hab. virg.*, c. 5 (*MPL*, IV, 445); cf. the entire passage, *MPL*, IV, 444-446. The virgins indeed wore a veil, and Tertullain wrote an entire treatise on the veiling of virgins (cf. *MPL*, II, 887-914), in which he expressly stated that in many churches this custom had an apostolic origin (*MPL*, II, 890). But as Muzzarelli states (*op. cit.*, p. 35), this veil seemed not at the time to differ from the ordinary veil of married women, and it probably served more as an external garment of modesty than as a distinguishing sign of their state.

(40) By *divine constitution* this is the only division of classes in the Church, the clergy by reason of the same divine institution being organized into a sacred hierarchy of orders, in which there is a subordination of one to another. Cf. Bouscaren-Ellis, *Canon Law, A Text*

correctly speak of the "canonical state of perfection" when referring to the religious life of that period. This is certainly true as regards the organized state which did not exist at the time, (41) and is no less true of the individual and personal pursuit of perfection which comprised *the* religious state of the period.

But the centuries which followed this sowing of the first seeds of the life of perfection produced such a rich harvest in the flower of the religious life, that ecclesiastical legislation could not be expected long to ignore its existence, and for the countless souls who showed themselves so eager to respond to Christ's great challenge of love, the Church, gradually and with care, developed the religious life by creating the *Religious State* (or even more precisely, the *Juridic Religious State*) in such a way as to facilitate this response. For recognizing not only the intrinsic worth and utility to the individual of a life which has perfection as its goal and the counsels as its means, but very much aware also of the contribution of such a life to the perfecting of the entire Body of which the individual is but a member, the Church zealously assumed protective legal custody of the state established by Christ and, with the essential elements of that state forming a solid framework, gave its approval to and fostered numerous other elements which have coalesced to provide a setting in which love can flourish generously, and which has redounded as well to the glory and welfare of both society and the Church as a whole, the resulting magnificent edifice of the juridic religious state comprising the second of the three principal ecclesiastical states in the Church today. (42) And among these "other elements" which contributed to the ultimate crystallization of this state in the year 1917, when the present Code of Canon Law was promulgated, none had greater effect historically than the institution of the common life and the role of the secondary ends of the religious life.

a. The common life.

To understand the development of the religious state into its present form, one must realize that from the beginning of the fourth century until the thir-

and Commentary (Milwaukee: Bruce, 1946), p. 358 (hereafter cited *Commentary*); Beste, *Introductio In Codicem* (3. ed., Collegeville, Minn.: St. John's Abbey Press, 1946), p. 166 (hereafter cited *Introductio*); cf. also cans. 107, 108.

(41) Although the first vestiges of the "common life" appear as early as the time of St. Cyprian, when many virgins were living under the special care and tutelage of the bishops (cf. *De hab. virg.*—*MPL*, IV, 445), and by the end of the third century there were community houses of virgins known as *παφθενωνας*, in which, it appears, young girls other than the "religious" also dwelt to receive their Christian education [cf. St. Athanasius, *Vita S. Antonii*, c. 3 (*MPG*, XXVI, 844); St. Ambrose referred to these houses as "*monasterium virginale*."—*De Lapsu Virginis*, VIII, c. 28 (*MPL*, XVI, 375)], aggregation to any society besides the Church (to which all Christians must adhere) was not known among the virgins and the ascetics.

(42) Cf. Pius XII, const. *Provida Mater Ecclesia*, 2 febr. 1947—*AAS*, XXXIX (1947), 116; can. 107. The other two principal states, as already seen, are the clerical and the lay, being found in the Church by divine institution.

teenth, when the Mendicant Orders made their appearance, the history of the religious life was essentially the history of monasticism. (43) During the persecutions of Decius (249-251), Valerian (253-260) and Diocletian (284-305), many men and women had taken refuge in the deserts, particularly in the deserts of Egypt, in order to escape persecution and more freely and safely to pursue perfection. As men gradually developed a sense of the superiority of renunciation as compared with self-indulgence, this eremitical form of life attracted more and more followers for its own sake, and from Egypt the movement spread to Palestine and Syria. By the middle of the fourth century, groups of these monks had inaugurated the cenobitic life in the usual sense of the word. (44) Its first vestiges, seen in the semi-erimitical type of life established by Saint Anthony (d.c. 356), (45) formed but a step to the cenobitic life as established by St. Pachomius (d. 346), (46) which in turn was rounded out and given impetus by St. Basil (c. 330-379) and so many other outstanding leaders of the East and the West. (47) But if the Abbey can be looked upon as the child of Saints Anthony, Pachomius and Basil, so also is it true that it became the ward even more completely of St. Benedict (480-547), who nurtured it in his twelve mother chapters

(43) The rise and the role of the monastic institutes in the history of the Church have been given detailed treatment in many fine works. Montalembert's *The Monks of the West* (2 vols., Boston, 1874) is a classic treatment of the subject. Cf. also McLaughlin, *Le Tres Ancien Droit Monastique de l'Occident* (Paris: Abbaye Saint-Martin, 1935). Brief but good accounts are to be found in many general histories of the Church. Cf. McSorley, *Outline History of the Church by Centuries* (4. ed., St. Louis: B. Herder, 1945), in the table of contents under "Communities." Cf. also *The Catholic Encyclopedia* (15 vols., 2 Supplements and Index, New York: Appleton Co., 1907-1922), in the articles: Religious; Monasticism; Pachomius, Saint; Basil the Great; Basil, Rule of Saint; Benedict of Nursia, Saint; Benedict, Rule of Saint; Benedictine Order; Cluny. Anderson (*op. cit., passim*) contains a fine appreciation. The brief outline presented here is a summary of some of the principal facts.

(44) "Coenobium," from κοινὸς βίος, "common life" is a word applied to a group, more or less numerous, living under a leader or abbot.

(45) Saint Anthony is often called the Father of Monasticism. Colonies of from two to ten monks lived under his leadership in separate cells and came together only at stated intervals for common worship. The life of St. Anthony, substantially accurate and probably written by St. Athanasius (c. 296-373), contains a good account of early monasticism in Egypt. Cf. *MPG*, XXVI, 835-978.

(46) St. Pachomius is generally conceded to be the Founder of Monasticism, and was the first legislator of the ascetic life in common. His nine monasteries for men and two for women, complete with a superior general and local superiors, formed the first monastic congregation.

(47) Among those of the East particular mention should be made of Saints Euthymius (d. 473), Sabas (439-532) and Nilus (d. 430); St. Athanasius (c. 296-373) and St. Ambrose in Italy, St. Augustine (354-430) in Africa, St. Martin (316-397), St. Honoratus (350-430), Cassian (360-435) in Gaul, St. Augustine (d. 604) in England, St. Boniface (c. 672/673-754) in Germany, St. Patrick (387-461) and St. Columban (543-615) in Ireland, are but a few of the outstanding men who figure prominently in the history of monasticism in the West.

into maturity, and the Benedictine movement spreading far and wide became one of the chief formative factors in the development not only of the religious life but of Europe itself.

Now the foundation and regulation of the first religious communities did not directly come about as the result of ecclesiastical legislation, but was of private initiative. What had begun as a personal, individual effort for the early masters of the desert, who had fled the world to embrace a life of seclusion, by force of circumstances became a social affair when, attracting large followings of disciples wishing to emulate them, these recognized masters of perfection found it necessary, in order to prevent a state of chaos, to draw up rules and regulations for the ordering of these groups. As long as these communities gave no evidence of any forms of abuse or disorder existing in their internal and external relationships—and such was apparently lacking in the beginning—the Church evidently did not find it necessary to legislate regarding them, and they therefore were not restricted in any manner, nor was it required by any general law that they have episcopal consent or sanction before being established. (48)

But along with the phenomenal growth of the monastic life there eventually did arise the need for the strong protective hand of ecclesiastical authority, and consequently the Council of Chalcedon in the year 451 explicitly legislated that no religious institute could thenceforth be founded or exist except under ecclesiastical jurisdiction. (49) Particularly for the purposes of this study, the

(48) This is not to say that the first monks and their foundations were not subject to the jurisdiction of the bishops. They were, as the lives of St. Anthony and St. Pachomius show. Pachomius established a number of foundations with the consent of the bishop of the place, and St. Athanasius, Patriarch of Alexandria, visited the monks of Egypt and praised and approved their way of life. In like manner, the monastic foundations of the West were either established by or at least subject to the jurisdiction of the bishops. In the early years of monastic life, however, such submission was probably due more to the monks' desire to cooperate with the bishops and to have their guidance and protection, than it was made necessary by specific legislation. Cf. Orth, *The Approbation of Religious Institutes*, The Catholic University of America Canon Law Studies, n. 71 (Washington, D. C.: The Catholic University of America, 1931), p. 12 hereafter cited Orth); *Kurtscheid, Historia Iuris Canonici, Historia Institutorum* (Vol. I, *Ab Ecclesiae Fundatione usque ad Gratianum*, Romae: Officium Libri Catholici, 1941), I, 177 (hereafter cited *Historia Institutorum*); Steiger, "De propagatione et diffusione vitae religiosae," *Periodica*, XIII (1924) (48).

(49) C. 4—Mansi, VII, 359. The canon was incorporated into the *Codex Iuris Civilis* of Justinian (*Novel.*, V, 1; CXXXI, 7) and was reiterated in the decrees of many particular councils throughout the world. Cf. the Council of Barcelona (541)—Mansi, IX, 109; Council of Agde (506), cc. 27, 58—Mansi, VIII, 330, 334; Council of Epaon (517), c. 10—Mansi, VIII, 560. Gratian has the substance of the law in his *Concordia Discordantium Canonum*, c. 10, C. XVIII, q. 2. [Gratian's monumental work is believed to have been completed about the year 1140. Cf. Van Hove, *Commentarium Lovaniense in Codicem Iuris Canonici*, Vol. I, Tom. I, *Prolegomena ad Codicem Iuris Canonici* (2. ed., Mechliniae-Romae: H. Dessain, 1945), p. 339 (hereafter cited *Prolegomena*)]. It is to be noted that *papal* approval of monastic institutes was not required by law until the IV Lateran Council (1215), episcopal sanction being sufficient until that time

effects of this piece of legislation cannot be overestimated: by that act the Church made the organized religious state completely its own, and since its ends therefore were sought and accomplished under the explicit approval of the Church, the members became more or less the Church's official representatives. Moreover, since thus the institutes themselves existed as ecclesiastical corporations, the inalienable right of supreme administrative power over them became resident in the Roman Pontiff (and subject to him and his restrictions, in the bishops throughout the world), and hence *his absolute control over them was limited only by natural justice and equity.*

The evolution saw its completion in the legislation of the thirteenth century. For while it is true that after the introduction of monasticism (50) the pursuit of evangelical perfection for the most part took place in monastic institutes, so that it is true to say that the history of the religious life up to the thirteenth century is essentially the history of monasticism, to assume that the Church recognized monasticism as the only juridic form of the religious life during the earlier period is to labor under a misconception. Neither *de iure* nor *de facto* was the juridic concept of "religious" limited to those who besides making profession were incorporated in an approved religious institute, but on the contrary the solitary pursuit of evangelical perfection was canonically recognized and approved by ecclesiastical authority during the entire period. (51) In the thirteenth century, however, the IV Lateran Council (1215), in order to counteract the confusion that was threatening the Church because of the great multiplication of orders, legislated that no new institute could be founded without papal approval, and that anyone wishing to enter a religious institute had to enter one of the already existing approved orders. (52) Coupling this legislation

(50) It may well be recalled here that from the very beginning the Monastic Life comprised in its membership both men and women. Already in the fourth century Egypt had as many monasteries for men as for women. Cf. Muzzarelli, p. 62, note 11; Kurtscheid, *Historia Institutorum*, p. 179.

(51) To this one can conclude by viewing ecclesiastical legislation beginning with the Council of Elvira (c. 305), which attached canonical effects to the virgins' vow of chastity (cf. c. 13—Bruns, *Canones Apostolorum et Conciliorum Saeculorum* IV-VII, [2 vols., Berolini, 1839] I, 4 [hereafter cited Bruns]), down through the regulations regarding the public taking of the veil contained in the II Council of Carthage in 390 (c. 3—Bruns, I, 118), the Roman Synod of the year 396/398? (c. 2—Mansi, III, 1134) and the letters of Pope Innocent I (402-417)—c. 9, 10, C. XXVII, q. 1 Cf. Jaffé, *Regesta Pontificum Romanorum ab condita Ecclesia ad annum post Christum natum* MCXCVIII (2. ed., correctam et auctam auspiciis Gulielmi Wattenbach curaverunt F. Kaltenbrunner, P. Ewald, S. Loewenfeld, 2 vols., in 1, Lipsiae, 1885-1888), JK, n. 286 (hereafter cited JE, JK, JL), and Pope Leo the Great (440-461)—c. 1, C. XX, q. 3; JK, n. 544, and Gratian's understanding of the institute—c. 7, C. XXVII, q. 1. Cf. also *glossa ordinaria* ad c. 7, C. XXVII, q. 1.

(52) C. 13—Mansi, XXII, 1002. There is no explicit mention in the law that the Holy See itself needed to give this approval, and neither is this explicitly mentioned in the Decretals of Gregory IX, where the Lateran decree is repeated (c. 9, X, *de religiosis domibus ut episcopo sint subjecti*, III, 36). But that this was the meaning of the law and was so understood

with a previous decision of the II Lateran Council that all religious vows were solemn (53) and the later declaration of Pope Boniface VIII (1294-1303) that those vows only were solemn which were either imposed by the reception of major orders, or which were freely made by profession in a religious order approved by the Holy See, (54) the conclusion logically follows: if to be a religious one needed to have solemn vows, and if solemn vows could be taken only in an order, then, to be a religious, one needed at the same time to be incorporated in an approved order. At least from the time of Pope Boniface VIII, therefore, if not indeed from the IV Lateran Council itself, the Church, while not condemning the solitary life, no longer accepted it as "religious," and the situation which could and did exist, whereby a religious did not necessarily form part of an approved institute, but was simply called professed or professed in such an institute or monastery, was no longer possible. (55)

Divinely and ecclesiastically constituted, therefore, the juridic religious state as it exists today had received its *essentially determining elements* in the thirteenth century, when to the primary end (perfection) and principal means (evangelical counsels) given it by Christ, the Church added the notion of the common life. From that time to the present, any state which does not include all of these elements cannot be recognized as the canonical state of religious perfection. (56) These elements, however, while absolutely essential to the juridic religious life, do not, and never have, precluded the simultaneous existence of secondary ends and means consistent with and serving complete dedication of the indi-

---

is easily seen. Commentators on the Decretals so interpreted it (cf. Hostiensis, *Commentaria in Quinque Decretalium Libros* [5 vols. in 3, Venetiis, 1581], on c. 9, X, III, 36, s.v. *approbatis*), and the II Council of Lyons (1274), when explicitly demanding the approbation of the Holy See, at the same time suppressed all the institutes established since the IV Lateran Council if they had not obtained papal approbation.—C. 23 (Mansi, XXIV, 96).

(53) Cc. 17, 18—Mansi, XXI, 527-528. It is not certain when the distinction between simple (non-invalidating) and solemn (invalidating) vows came into being, but the distinction was certainly common in the thirteenth century. The use of the terms simple and solemn are found for the first time in the *Decree* of Gratian; they were used in the schools of Canon Law of the time and were officially adopted by the Roman Pontiffs. Cf. c. 8, D. XXVII; c. 5, X, *de statu monachorum et canonicorum regularium*, III, 35; c. 20, X, *de conversione coniugatorum*, III, 32; c. 3, 6, 7, X, *qui clerici vel voventes matrimonium contrahere possunt*, IV, in VI°. For a treatment of the history of this matter cf. Frey, *The Act of Religious Profession*, The Catholic University of America Canon Law Studies, n. 63 (Washington, D. C.: The Catholic University of America, 1931), pp. 31-47.

(54) C. un., *de voto et voti redemptione*, III, 15, in VI°.

(55) Cf. Schaefer, *De Religiosis*, p. 58; Wernz, *Ius Decretalium*, III, n. 590; Bouix, *De Jure Regularium*, I, 207-208; *Larraona*, "Commentarium Codicis," *CpR*, II (1921), 137.

(56) Cf. cans. 487, 488, 1°.; Pius XII, const. *Provida Mater Ecclesia*, 2 febr. 1947—*AAS*, XXXIX (1947), 120. It is interesting to note that in the first drafts of canon 487, the element of the "common life" is not explicitly mentioned, but is included only in the final revision. Cf. *Schema Codicis Iuris Canonici* (ed. cum notis Petri Card. Gasparri, Romae, 1912), canon 368.

vidual to the love of God. It was in fact the recognition by the Holy See of the important role of the secondary ends in the religious life that prompted a revision of the juridic concept of that state itself.

b. The secondary ends of the religious state.

From the time of Pachomius, who in his Rule wisely and accurately determined the manner of life for his monks in a community, (57) within a cloister, (58) under obedience (59) and in poverty, (60) the pursuit of perfection in community life through the observance of the three vows (61) of poverty, chastity and obedience was of the very essence of the life of every community. This and this alone made a monk to be a monk, and the differences in the *modus vivendi* followed in the various communities did not make a member of one community any more or less of a religious than the member of any other.

But if differences among the various communities can be expected, they are certainly to be found in the history of monasticism. From its inception, the religious life exhibited a rich variety of spiritual trends and modes. For although each institute was found with the common purpose to create and perfect in its members the perfect image of Christ through the observance of the evangelical counsels, for the attaining of this objective each was found also to have its own unique spirit, its own manner of approach, which distinguished it and set it apart from all the rest. Special mortifications and practices, long prayers and frequent vigils, strict fasts, total abstinence from meat, perpetual silence, and other ascetical practices, were recognized as being accidental concomitances of a *particular* form of the religious life, the severity of such austerities differing from community to community and from age to age.

And no less a divergence arose from the variety of occupations in which the monks engaged. They became the pioneers of Christian civilization. They preached the Gospel, served the poor and the sick, instructed the young in religion and in the various arts and crafts. Working as copyists, they preserved for posterity the Scriptures, the writings of the Fathers, and many literary treasures of classical antiquity. In short, the abbey became the center of culture, crafts, church ceremonial, scholarship, aesthetics, medicine and agriculture, and the faithful soon learned to turn to it in almost every need and affliction of soul and body.

---

(57) *Reg. Pachomius*, cc. 16, 20, 21, 156 (*MPL*, XXIII, 67, 80).

(58) *Ibidem*, cc. 52, 54, 84, 108, 136, 137 (*MPL*, XXIII, 71, 72, 74, 75).

(59) *Ibidem*., cc. 157, 158 (*MPL*, XXIII, 80).

(60) *Ibidem*, cc. 81, 83 (*MPL*, XXIII, 73, 74).

(61) The act of profession in the Rule of St. Pachomius was more or less a private act. His monks did not explicitly emit a formal vow; a change of secular garment for the monastic habit was the only external sign showing that one had taken upon himself the obligations of the religious state. Cf. *Reg. Pachomii* c. 49 (*MPL*, XXIII, 700; cf. also Steiger, "De propagatione et diffusione vitae religiosae," *Periodica*, XIII (1924) (48).

But no matter how rounded and agreeably varied became his regimen, the main purpose of the monk continued to be the perfecting of himself for the indwelling of God's spirit. His charities and services were many, but for thirteen centuries they were restricted to the persons dwelling within the abbey walls or in the vicinity; they did not extend beyond the monastery circle. With the growth and development of town life, however, there arose a new social structure which, along with its advantages, contained some not too pleasant features, such as pestilence, vice or poverty, calling for religious ministrations other than such as were required by the people dwelling near the great monastic establishments. St. Francis of Assisi (1128-1226) and St. Dominic (1170-1221), to meet the challenge of the times, founded the first two orders of mendicants, (62) true religious societies complying with the juridical requirements of the period, with the secondary end of devotion and service to the inhabitants of towns and cities. The foundation of many other mendicant religious societies rapidly followed, and, existing side by side with the great monastic foundations, these groups performed a wonderful service, particularly in the fields of education, of social service, of the conversion of heretics, and of a preaching and missionary activity. (63)

Particularly the period following the Council of Trent witnessed the establishment of almost an innumerable number of institutes dedicated to the profession of Christian perfection, but also devoted in a special way to the effective service of society, of the Church and of its members, and exercising a varied apostolate and ministry in a considerable variety of forms. The religious state thus beneficially contributed not only to the life of the individual seeking perfection, but also to the life of society and of the Church as a whole. For all this there was official recognition and praise. The "splendor and usefulness" accruing to the Church of God from the well-regulated existence of religious institutes (64) was frequently and explicitly acknowledged by the Roman Pontiffs, and this especially as, with the passing of the years, the increasing good

(62) Mendicants, in the strict sense, are the members of those institutes which according to Rule or constitution are unable to possess anything, even in common, either movable or immovable, as their own. Wherefore they live the uncertain life of a beggar, the word mendicant being the English equivalent of the Latin participle of *mendicare*, to beg. Up to the Council of Trent (1545-1563) there were many mendicant orders in the strict sense, but that council allowed all but the Friars Minor of the strict observance and the Capuchins to own *bona immobilia* (sess. XXV, *de regularibus*, c. 3), the named institutes remaining to this day the only mendicant orders in the strict sense. In the broad sense, those institutes are called mendicant which in their foundation were by Rule or constitution unable to possess anything as their own, but which provision has since been mitigated or dispensed from, either by the concession of the Council of Trent, or by Apostolic Privilege. Cf. Schaefer, *De Religiosis*, p. 86.

(63) Cf. McSorley, *Outline History of the Church by Centuries*, pp. 398-401.

(64) Cf. Conc. Trident., sess. XXV, *de regularibus*, c. 1.

accomplished by these institutes became more and more manifest. (65) Indeed, as mentioned above, it was the recognition by the Holy See of the important role of the secondary ends in the religious life that brought about a modification of the juridic concept of the state.

It is to be recalled that the legislation of the thirteenth century, when determining the constitutive elements of the religious state, not only decreed the necessity of the common life, but likewise laid down the principle that only those societies had ecclesiastical approval in which solemn vows were taken. The comparatively severe life of these orders, however, which generally also included the observance of the cloister, did not allow them to give to society all that multifarious service which Christian charity inspires, and so, as Pope Pius X (1903-1914) wrote in 1906 when reviewing the history of the religious state, to adequately meet the needs of the times, Divine Providence inspired the founding of societies of men and women which, while still preserving the true nature of the religious state, by their more lenient rules were also able to participate in many works of religion and charity not readily accessible to the institutes following the ancient and established mode of the religious life. (66)

These societies, or congregations as they soon came to be canonically known, (67) differed from the religious orders particularly in the profession of simple vows taken by the *sodales*, and since simple profession, whether by men or women, was directly contrary to the express wishes of the Holy See as manifested in explicit legislation, (68) it can readily be understood why the rise and official recognition of the congregations was at first attended with many difficulties and obstacles. (69) But the demonstrated ability of these societies to

---

(65) In his encyclical letter *Ubi primum* (June 17, 1847), written on the occasion of the institution of the *Congregatio super Statu Regularium*, Pope Pius IX (1846-1878) beautifully summed up the Holy See's traditional appreciation of this role played by the religious state. Cf. Bizzarri, *Collectanea in Usum Secretariae Sacrae Congregationis Episcoporum et Regularium* (ed. noviss., Romae, 1885), pp. 868-869 (hereafter cited *Collectanea*).

(66) Motu propr. *Dei providentis*, 16 iul. 1906—*Acta Sanctae Sedis* (41 vols., Romae, 1865-1908), XXXIX (1906), 344 (hereafter cited *ASS*).

(67) The ecclesiastical approval of one of the first of these societies so specified it. Cf. Const. *Ex commissa*, 22 sept. 1655—*Bullarum Diplomatum et Privilegiorum Sanctorum Romanorum Pontificum Taurinensis Editio* (25 vols., Augustae Taurinorum, 1857-1872), XVI, 67 (hereafter cited *Bull. Rom. Taur.*).

(68) There could be no misunderstanding the mind of Pope Pius V (1566-1572), for example, with regard to this matter. Cf. his Constitution *Circa pastoralis*, 29 maii 1566—*Codicis Iuris Canonici Fontes*, cura Emi Petri Card. Gasparri editi (9 vols., Romae [postea Civitate Vaticana]: Typis Polyglottis Vaticanis, 1923-1939; [Vols. VII-IX ed. cura et studio Emi Iustiniani Card. Serédi], n. 112 (hereafter cited *Fontes*), and the Bull *Lubricum vitae genus*, 17 nov. 1568—*Bull. Rom. Taur.*, VII, 725.

(69) "Non nisi paulatim admodum et per gradus, sensim sive sensu ac furtim fere, Congregationes, mulierum praesertim initio non una de causa aversatae, aegre toleratae postea, dein permissae, laudatae paulo post ac demum plene approbatae, Religionibus proprie dictis aequiparatae quadantenus fuerunt ac religiosi iuris, exceptis semper privilegiis, par-

meet the exigencies of the times, for which the austere rules of the existing Orders could not well provide, gradually overcame the reluctance of the Church to recognize their place in the canonical state of perfection. Many individual congregations rising under Episcopal authorization soon gained pontifical approval as early as the latter half of the sixteenth century, (70) and the succeeding years witnessed an ever increasing number of such papally approved religious institutes of simple vows, their status, privileges, rights and exemptions following not from the common law, however, but from the particular indults of approval. It remained for Pope Leo XIII (1878-1903) in his Apostolic Constitution *Conditae a Christo* (Dec. 8, 1900) to give the congregations a permanent and specific standing in the common law of the Church as canonical states of perfection, (71) his immortal work being perfected by the Code of Canon Law, which admitted congregations of simple vows among religious institutes in the strict sense. (72)

Such, then, in its main elements, was the evolution of the religious state as established by Christ into the religious state as it exists today, a juridic institute of the Church. Comparatively a considerable amount of space has been given to this outline because, while it is vocation to the religious state in its present form that is the chief concern of this study, as will be seen, that concept will be understood in a much clearer light when viewed with relation to the development as well as the crystallized nature of the state presently existing.

2. Some precisions on the nature of the juridic religious state.

As succinctly defined by the Church in the Code of Canon Law, the religious state now exists as a firmly established manner of living in community, by which the faithful, in a society approved by legitimate ecclesiastical authority, strive after evangelical perfection by undertaking to observe not only the ordinary precepts, but also, according to the laws proper to their society, the evangelical counsels, by means of the public vows (73) of obedience, chastity, and poverty, the vows being either perpetual or temporary, the latter to be renewed at the time of their expiration. (74) The primary end and essential means of the religious state, therefore, have never changed: they remain the pursuit of personal

ticipes effectae."—Larraona, "Commentarium," *CpR*, I (1920), 46. Cf. also Freriks, *Religious Congregations in Their External Relations*, The Catholic University Canon Law Studies, n. 1 (Washington, D. C.: The Catholic University of America, 1916), pp. 16-32 (hereafter cited *Religious Congregations*).

(70) Cf. Freriks, *Religious Congregations*, p. 22; Larraona, "Commentarium," *ibidem*, pp. 48-49, and references to documents of erection there cited.

(71) *Fontes*, n. 644.

(72) Cf. Pius XII, const. *Provida Mater Ecclesia*, 2 febr. 1947—*AAS*, XXXIX (1947), 116-117; can. 488, 2°.

(73) That is, made *in facie ecclesiae*, received by a legitimate superior who is recognized by the Church as being capable of accepting the vows *in nomine Ecclesiae*. Cf. can. 1308, 1°.

(74) Cf. cans. 487, 488, 1°.

sanctification through the three vows of poverty, chastity and obedience. (75) The point needs special emphasis, for it is a truth in our pragmatic times that there is a tendency to justify religious life on wrong principles, even to minimize its essentials and to emphasize the accidentals. Often enough one hears it said that teaching or nursing religious are of great value to the Church, but what is the value of the cloistered life? Obviously the emphasis is on the activity of teaching or nursing; the "religious element" becomes an efficient adjunct to the activity. Indeed it is a fact that the secondary ends of the religious state have played such a prominent role in that life, particularly after the Council of Trent, that they have become in the mind of society at large its most distinguishing characteristic and so stand out that, in the minds of many, they all but obscure its primary end. This is unfortunate, because it has led to a distorted concept of the true nature of the religious state which, as has been seen, is of great value to every member of the Mystical Body.

The fact does remain, however, that the religious of today are most closely and officially associated in a special way with the many charitable and educational works of the Church, and this *de iure* as well as *de facto*. (76) Indeed, the secon-

---

(75) "Finis cuiuslibet Religionis, sive agatur de Ordinibus sive de Congregationibus, est sanctificatio personalis, idest christiana Sodalium perfectio seu divina caritas . . . media essentialia ad hunc finem assequendum sunt tria vota obedientiae, castitatis, paupertatis."—Schaefer, *De Religiosis*, p. 30.

(76) As regards the *de facto* given recognition, the matter is evident and needs no belaboring. Non-Catholics as well as Catholics have learned to turn to the heroic souls of Religion in almost every need and affliction of soul and body, and particularly have the various fields of education, missionary activity and social service (the care of the aged, the infirm, the homeless, etc.) profited by the outstanding and wonderful work of these institutes. While it would be apropos to illustrate the fact with at least a brief account of their foundation and history, their very number places even a complete listing of them outside the scope of this study. For a synopsis of the history and the work of sixty-two orders and congregations of men and one hundred and fifty congregations of women before the Code of Canon Law, the reader is referred to the two volumes of H. Hohn, *Vocations, Conditions of Admission, etc., into the Monasteries, Congregations, Societies, Religious Institutes, etc., According to Authentical Information and the Latest Regulations* (New York: Benziger, 1910), and *Vocations, Conditions of Admission*, etc., *into the Convents, Congregations, Societies, Religious Institutes, According to Authentical Information and the Latest Regulations* (New York: Benziger, 1912). Cf. also the listing and statistics contained in Schaefer, *De Religiosis*, pp. 23-30, 92-94; *CpRM*, XXII (1931), 314-320. Vocation pamphlets also sometimes carry a listing of religious orders and congregations. Cf., for example, Heck, *Christ Calls* (St. Meinrad, Indiana: St. Meinrad's Abbey Press, 1945), which not only lists ninety religious institutes of men and two hundred sixty five religious societies of women to be found in the United States, but also gives information regarding the various types of activities in which each group engages.

With regard to the *de iure* recognized association, one of the very first matters the Congregation of Religious wishes to be informed about when application is made for the foundation of a new institute is the nature of the good works the proposed congregation wishes to engage in (cf. S. C. de Religiosis, *Normae*, 6 mart. 1921 [Romae: Typis Polyglottis Vaticanis, 1922], cap. I, n. 4), and approval of the congregation carries with it *ipso facto* the ap-

dary ends of the various religious institutes have the greatest single influence on the total organization of these institutes, (77) and when it is realized that these ends are sought and accomplished under the explicit approval of the Church by a special ecclesiastical order of canonical persons, juridically recognized and privileged and therefore more or less official representatives of the Church, it is easily seen how the good which religious accomplish, and, conversely, the scandal to which at times they may give rise, redounds in a most special way to the glory or to the harm of the Church itself. Bearing the Church's stamp of approval, religious are known as a group set apart: through their profession, by which act they are made members of a unique ecclesiastical class, they obtain special and public deputation to divine worship and are publicly revered as sacred persons, (78) and for so many they represent *the* educational and charitable activity of the Church. This fact shall be seen to be of the greatest importance when explicit attention is given to vocation to the religious state.

Of hardly less importance to that concept, it will be seen, is the element of common life as it pertains to the essential nature of that state. For by religious profession, as has been pointed out, there arises a social element, or bond, by which a person is joined to a specific institute, and incorporated in it as a member. Without it the canonical state of religious perfection today does not exist. Therefore, in the profession of vows, besides the juridically recognized spiritual and unilateral quasi-contract which arises between the individual and God, (79) there is implicitly contained another contract, a human bond, bilateral in character, which immediately sets up a whole series of reciprocal rights and duties on the part of the religious and the society to which he adheres. (80) This follows from the very nature of society itself, and since the religious family in which profession is made is an *ecclesiastical* institute, the contract by that very fact is also between the religious and the Church, which, therefore, is entitled completely to govern it. (81)

---

proval of those secondary ends. Also much of the legislation of the Church with respect to religious has direct reference to the secondary aims of the life. Cf., for example, can. 497, 2°-3°, and Stenger ("Canonical Episcopal Visitation of Religious Communities," *The Jurist* [Washington, D. C., 1941—], II [1942], Supplement to the July issue) illustrates how many of the canonical questions which must be asked on the occasion of a bishop's visitation of religious institutes have to do with the secondary ends of those institutes.

(77) Cf. Schaefer, *De Religiosis*, p. 31.

(78) Cf. Schaefer, *De Religiosis*, p. 36.

(79) Coronata, *Institutiones*, I, n. 589.

(80) Cf. Creusen-Garesché-Ellis, *Religious Men and Women in the Code* (4. English ed., Milwaukee: Bruce, 1942), n. 222; Vermeersch-Creusen, *Epitome Iuris Canonici* (3 vols., 6. ed., Mechliniae-Romae: Dessain, 1937-1946), I, n. 722 (hereafter cited *Epitome*); Goyeneche, *Iuris Canonici Summa Principia, De Religiosis* (Romae: *Commentarium Pro Religiosis*, 1938), n. 62 (hereafter cited *De Religiosis*).

(81) Wernz-Vidal, *De Religiosis*, p. 10, nota (14); cf. also Creusen-Garesché-Ellis, *loc. cit.*, " . . . it (religious profession) establishes a new bond of dependence in regard to the hierarchy."

On the basis of this contract, the religious voluntarily subjects himself to the society and binds himself to live in conformity with the rules and regulations of that institute with regard to both spiritual and temporal matters, transferring to it the right to utilize his faculties of soul and body. (82) Living together under the same roof with his fellow religious and having a common participation in the ordinary needs of life, he likewise is bound to have a courteous and complaisant regard and consideration for them. The institute, on the other hand, is obliged to direct the religious in things spiritual, through the manner of life proper to the respective institute and under the guidance of competent superiors, as well as to provide him with whatever is necessary in the way of support, food, clothing, lodging, etc. In short, it is to treat him after the manner of a son. (83) Moreover, by his profession the religious becomes the recipient of many privileges not enjoyed by the laity, both those which the Holy See has directly conceded to his particular institute and the privileges enumerated in the common law of the Church. (84)

It is definitely a state with a religio-social nature, therefore, a state completely under the jurisdiction of the Church, about which an individual is inquiring when he asks "Have I a religious vocation?" And it is exactly the same state which this study has in view when it seeks the answer to the age-old question, "What is the nature of a religious vocation? Is it divine? ecclesiastical? or a combination of both?" (85)

---

(82) Wernz-Vidal, *De Religiosis*, n. 300; Coronata, *loc. cit.;* O'Neill, *The Dismissal of Religious in Temporary Vows*, The Catholic University of America Canon Law Studies, n. 166 (Washington, D. C.: The Catholic University of America Press, 1942), p. 73.

(83) Wernz-Vidal, *loc. cit.;* Coronata, *loc. cit.;* Goyeneche, *loc. cit.*

(84) Cf. cans. 613, 614.

(85) Attention is here drawn to the fact that in the Church today others besides religious in the strict sense are recognized members of the canonical state of perfection. For there are certain approved societies in the Church, both of men and of women, whose members strive after perfection by leading a community life after the manner of religious, but who do not take the usual vows of religion (that is, *public* vows), and therefore, while they do not form part of the religious state in its juridic sense (cf. cans. 673; 487, 488, 1°), these societies receive mention in the Code of Canon Law under the general section treating of the religious state (cans. 673-681) and are true units within the juridic state of perfection. They come under the jurisdiction of the Sacred Congregation of Religious and much of the general legislation on the religious state pertains also to them. The members of such societies are popularly known as "quasi-religious." In addition, a recent enactment of the present Holy Father has now given canonical standing in the state of perfection to the so-called "Secular Institutes," which had their origins in the middle of the last century. (Cf. const. *Provida Mater Ecclesia*, 2 febr. 1947—*AAS*, XXXIX [1947], 114-124). For a short treatment of the history and nature of these institutes cf. Woywod, *A Practical Commentary on the Code of Canon Law* (revised and enlarged edition, 2 vols., New York: John F. Wagner, 1948), I, 339-341 (hereafter cited *Commentary*). More than mere common associations of the faithful, these Secular Institutes are not religious organizations even on the plane of the "quasi-religious" societies, for while the members undertake to exercise the apostolate and to strive after perfection by following

a rule of life and by promising through private vow or oath to observe the evangelical counsels of perfect chastity, obedience and poverty (or at least the restricted use of property within the limits of the constitutions of the institute), the common life is not imposed on the members. They do now, however, form part of the juridic state of perfection along with the religious and "quasi-religious" institutes of the Church, and are also under the jurisdiction of the Congregation of Religious. Because much that is contained in the concept of religious vocation is directly applicable to these other two states of canonical perfection, reference shall be made to them by way of analogy when there will be treated specifically the subject proper to this study. It shall be seen that the concepts do not essentially differ.

CHAPTER IV

THE DIVINE VOCATION TO THE JURIDIC RELIGIOUS STATE

ARTICLE I. DIVINE VOCATION: ITS GENERIC NATURE AND NECESSITY

There certainly exists no difficulty about the *reality* of a divine vocation, the summons of divine mercy, where the question of licit entrance into the religious state is concerned. Anyone who has but the faintest notion of the religious life (in either its primordial or juridic sense) and even the most fundamental knowledge of theology, must admit that only an internal grace can account for one's intention rising above the legitimate attractions of earth to reason efficaciously to the desirability of the evangelical counsels. (1) For it has been seen in the preceding chapter that the primary goal towards which a subject is directed by a religious vocation is definitely on a supernatural level, the state of higher perfection, a perfection consisting in the closest conformity to the image and likeness of Christ and having its complete fruition in the union of the Beatific Vision in Heaven. Consequently, in virtue of the common principle that the means must be proportioned to the ends, the intention of a man to achieve that supernatural state, i.e., the efficacious motions of his intellect and will towards the supernatural goal, must itself be the effect of a supernatural principle, in short the work of divine grace. (2) For Saint Thomas, this "*propositum religionis assumendae*" (3) has as its principle, or is the elicited act of, one of the

(1) *Licit* entrance into the religious state is emphasized, for it is a fact, unhappily substantiated by history, that certain individuals, particularly in times past, have by valid profession in a canonical institute become religious through perverse motives, to escape punishment for crimes committed, for example, or to be well provided for as to temporalities. This unsavory matter will be treated in its proper place.

(2) "Holiness begins from Christ; and Christ is its cause. For no act conducive to salvation can be performed unless it proceeds from Him as from its supernatural source . . . It is He who through His heavenly grace is the principle of every supernatural act in all parts of the Body."—Pius XII, ep. encycl. *Mystici Corporis*, 29 iun. 1943—*AAS*, XXXV (1943), 216, 219 (NCWC translation, n. 51 and n. 57, pp. 20 and 22).

(3) Whenever Saint Thomas speaks of religious vocation in its passive modality, i.e., as a result produced in man corresponding to God's movement, in every instance he uses the phrase "*propositum religionis* (*assumendae*)," the "intention to embrace the religious life." In other words, the expression of religious vocation *in man* is, for Saint Thomas, an act of intention. Cf. his work "Contra Pestiferam Doctrinam Retrahentium Homines a Religionis Ingressu"—*Opuscula Selecta, Opusculum XVII* (Tom. III, Parisiis: Sumptibus et Typis P. Letheilleux, Editoris, 1881), pp. 1-58, especially cc. 9 & 10, pp. 24-34 (hereafter cited *Contra retrahentes*); cf. also *Summa Theologica*, IIa, IIae, q. 189, a. 10, ad 1; Farrell, *Theology of Religious Vocation*, pp. 75-76, 92, 152, 155, 158-159. The last named work, already referred to above, is a most excellent analysis of the Thomistic concept of religious vocation and is in-

infused supernatural virtues, (4) specifically and radically the virtue of religion, (5) specifically and actually an act of devotion (the primary and universal act of the virtue of religion), (6) and this in a most intense degree (7) and magnanimous mode. (8) Naturally, according to the order of causality, an actual grace which reduces the virtue of religion in such a way that there is effected the resultant act of devotion constituting religious vocation in its passive modality is also called for. (9)

Divine vocation, therefore, is a necessary theological conclusion in the question of licit entrance into the religious state. Considered under the aspect of a result produced in the one called, it is seen primarily as an efficacious intention to embrace the religious life ("*propositum religionis assumendae*"), an intense act of devotion in a magnanimous mode; (10) in its active modality, the divine call is viewed as God inviting someone, by an operation of grace upon the soul, to desire and to seek the religious state and, depending upon the text of the Scriptures or the writings of the Fathers he is citing, is variously described by Saint Thomas as an internal inspiration, an impetus of grace, a revelation of the Holy Spirit suggesting what men must do, an instinct of the Holy Spirit

---

valuable not only for its ordering and crystallization of the vast body of Thomistic teaching on religious vocation, scattered throughout his theological and polemical works, but also for its concrete applications of these principles to practical cases.

(4) Farrell, *op. cit.*, pp. 90-91.

(5) *Ibid.*, pp. 91-92.

(6) *Ibid.*, pp. 92-94.

(7) *Ibid.*, pp. 96-103.

(8) *Ibid.*, pp. 158-159; cf. also pp. 128-142, 155-159, where the author particularly demonstrates his thesis that without the virtue of magnaminity, the virtue which tends to great and difficult things, religious vocation is impossible.

(9) *Ibid.*, pp. 125-126.

(10) The qualifying adverb "primarily" is inserted here because, as shall be seen particularly with regard to the canonical religious state, the fact that God in his foreknowledge and consequent will predisposes an individual to possess the natural qualifications demanded by the Church at the time of his reception (health, talents, etc.) is a remote and more or less indirect preparation of the person, and in a wide but true sense may be looked upon as constituting part of the divine invitation to the religious state. For while an individual might be prompted by grace to have the "*propositum religionis assumendae*," no one could say that he was given a divine religious vocation if God permits the frustration of the carrying out of his intention by some cause incapacitating him in some way. The person will be rewarded for his good intention, a supernaturally meritorious act, for God often suggests plans which he does not require or desire to be carried into effect, though he is preparing the reward which He will bestow on the intention and the trial, but definitely no divine call to the juridic religious state has been given to one who, for example, has been born with a physical handicap which debars his entrance into that life. Likewise it should not be overlooked that other subjective factors, certain good habits, dispositions, and gifts of grace, contribute to a candidate's suitability for the religious state, and therefore can be considered under the aspect of divine vocation in its passive modality. On this latter point, cf. Farrell, *op. cit.*, pp. 142-150.

by which men are moved to enter religion, and an illuminating of reason. (11) In this sense the reality and necessity of a divine religious vocation must be admitted by all, and even Canon Lahitton, who is recognized as the great proponent of the theory which holds to the exclusive position of the external ecclesiastical call in the matter of religious vocation, finds no cause to dispute the fact. He merely thinks such an interior invitation calls for too subtle an investigation to give rise to practical concern, (12) arguing moreover that to call vocation a grace adds nothing real to the concept. (13)

Legal recognition of this divine vocation to the religious life is, of course, not wanting. Although an evident reality, the legislator on numerous occasions has seen fit to impress upon man the supernatural aspect of a call to the religious state, and for the purpose of this study his recognition of the fact is specifically pertinent. To avoid needless repetition, however, the investigation of these relevant texts is postponed until the following article, when they are seen in the light of the controversial question, "To whom is the divine vocation given? To all, or to just a designated few?"

Article II. Divine Vocation: The Quantitative Problem

The difficulty in the matter of divine religious vocation, then, lies not in the necessity and the generic quality of God's call to the religious state, but in its *quantitative conception*, a question which has its roots buried deep in the age-old problem of the specific nature of grace, predestination and free will, a source of perennial conflict between the various schools of theology. The problem, however, while strictly theological, is not the concern of the theologian alone, for its answer is of the utmost importance to the canonist as well. For obviously the religious state, particularly as it exists today, is not to be indiscriminately opened to all, a fact which sad experience has but emphasized. Now if the reason for a discrimination, or at least a partial reason, is to be found in the *certain fact* that God has restricted His call to the religious life, so that only a designated few have been singled out by His grace in preference to all others, then it is certainly the duty of the legislator to take cognizance of that fact and command those whose responsibility it is to admit worthy aspirants, to accept only those

(11) Cf. *Contra retrahentes*, c. 9, pp. 24-31, *passim*.

(12) Cf. Lahitton, *La Vocation Sacerdotale* (nouvelle edition, Paris, 1913), p. 96. "Cette découverte d'un appel interieur passif, on le voit, ne s'offre pas d'elle-même; elle est le fruit d'une investigation théologique assez subtile, et, nous le constaterons, mon moins inutile au point de vue practique."

(13) "Maintenant, cet appel interieur passif, que surajoute-t-il dans le sujet aux réalités que nous avons signalées comme necessaires? Rien absolutment rien. Quand donc le théologien, ami de speculation, donne à ce surnaturel . . . le nom d'appel divin passif, vocatio, c'est là une elucidation théologique, qui n'ajoute rien de reel. Au point de vue réel, il y a coincidence parfaite, identité absolue entre l'appel passif et la grâce, infusée dans l'ame, qui détrempe l'acte humain en vu d'un but supernaturel."—*Ibid.*, p. 97. Canon Lahitton's theory on religious vocation shall be seen in the article immediately following.

who show some favorable and positive manifestation of special divine predilection to that life. He would otherwise be remiss in carrying out the obligations of his office, for as has been pointed out, "the institutions of canon law teach the positive determinations which have been adopted from dogmatic and moral theology." (14) But if, on the other hand, God has issued a general vocation (at least relatively considered), whereby all men are radically capable of embracing that state, then both the legislator and the admitting superior must rely exclusively on other norms of discrimination. The "General-Special Divine Vocation Problem," therefore, enjoys a priority of first rank in any discussion of religious vocation, indeed it presents itself as the very core of the question. It has also presented anything but an easy solution.

1. The problem in its historical conspectus.

To anyone who is at all familiar with the controversy that has been waged since the seventeenth century concerning the precise nature and extension of God's call to the religious state, and is likewise aware that a solution in the speculative order is not in the foreseeable future, it may seem strange that the matter did not previously give rise to as great divergencies of opinion. It is a truth, however, that the problem was not acute in the Church for many centuries, and it is not without justification that modern day proponents of the universal-vocation theory ("the path of the evangelical counsels is open to all and may be urged upon all who have the requisite freedom and fitness to embrace them") appeal in support of their teaching to the well-nigh unanimous doctrine of the Fathers and theologians of the middle ages. The entire matter is perhaps best viewed in the light of the development seen in the preceding chapter.

In the first place, there is no doubt that Christ issued an external invitation to all men to follow the way of perfection by observing the counsels. His words to the young man of the Gospels were equally addressed to men of all ages, as Saint Thomas clearly shows:

> Let us see whether the counsel given to the youth by Our Lord, Matth. XIX, 21: *If thou wilt be perfect, go, sell what thou hast, and give to the poor*, was directed to him alone or also to all men. We can settle this question on the basis of the incidents which follow in the Gospel. For, when Peter said to Him: *Behold, we have left all and followed thee*, Our Lord fixed a reward for all, saying: *Everyone who has left house, or brothers etc., for my name's sake, shall receive a hundredfold, and shall possess life everlasting*. Hence, this counsel ought to be accepted by each individual no less than if it were offered to each individually from the mouth of Our Lord Himself. . . . Likewise, although He addressed the words to the young man as to a single individual, elsewhere he offered the same counsel universally, saying in Matth. XVI, 24: *If anyone wishes to come after me, let him deny himself*. . . . Consequently, the counsel given by the Lord to the youth is to be accepted as if proposed to all by the mouth of the Lord. (15)

---

(14) Yelle, *Travail Scientifique en Disciplines Ecclésiastiques*, p. 38.

(15) *Contra retrahentes*, c. 9, pp. 26-27.

Now in face of this universal external call and in view of the nature of the religious life as it was seen to have existed during the first three centuries, being as yet neither a juridic state nor even an organized social state, (16) it perhaps is not too surprising to discover that the idea of only a designated number of Christians being invited to pursue evangelical perfection, to the exclusion of others, seems altogether foreign to the thinking of the period. The writings of the Fathers simply praise that life and direct how it is to be lived and properly ordered, without limiting it to anyone, (17) and the only concept of vocation to the religious life apparent in this period is that which sees this state as open to every Christian who, heeding the invitation of Christ, can expect the grace to embrace it, a concept which finds exact expression in the ancient (circa 218) (18) *Traditio Apostolica*, when Saint Hippolytus wrote that "personal choice [προαίρεσις] (or one's own free will) alone is that which makes a virgin." (19)

It may be rather surprising, however, to find that this concept retained all but unanimous approval for many centuries, particularly in view of the fact that from the very beginning of the organized state of the religious life, and most especially from the time when the Church made that state completely its own, admission into it was on a definitely discriminatory basis. (20) And yet this appears to be the case. If the writers on the religious state recognized the basis for discrimination among religious candidates to arise out of a *special divine* predilection, granting the grace of vocation to some and denying it to others, then not only did they fail to voice their belief, but in their explicit statements they seemed to misrepresent their convictions. The great monastic founders, Saints Pachomius, Basil and Benedict, while they exhibited evident concern in their Rules that only the fit and worthy be admitted into their institutes, nowhere imposed upon superiors the obligation of discerning the *special* determining hand of Providence, selecting some and not others. (21) Moreover the early practice of parents offering their children while still in infancy to the service of God in the monastic life, and binding them there absolutely and per-

---

(16) Cf. *supra*, pp. 18-21.

(17) Cf. the passages cited *supra*, p. 20, notes (35), (39).

(18) For this date cf. Van Hove, *Prolegomena*, p. 125.

(19) Dix, *The Treatise on the Apostolic Tradition of St. Hippolytus of Rome* (New York: The Macmillan Co., 1937), p. 21 (hereafter cited *Apostolic Tradition*). "It is now generally recognized that the 'Apostolic Tradition' of St. Hippolytus is the most illuminating single source of evidence extant on the inner life and religious polity of the early Christian Church."—*Ibidem*, (IX).

(20) This point comprises the subject matter of the following chapter and shall there be considered in detail.

(21) Cf. *Reg. S. Pachomii*—*MPL*, XXXIII, 70; *Reg. Fus. S. Basilii, tract.* 10—*MPG*, XXXI, 943-947; *Reg. S. Benedicti*, c. 58—*MPL*, LXVI, 803. It is true that Saint Benedict gave the admonition "*Probate spiritus, si ex Deo sunt*," but in the context of the chapter the phrase obviously has reference to the sincere and supernatural intention which every aspirant to the religious life must have.

petually, continued through almost eight centuries of the Church's history as a legitimately recognized custom, (22) and points to a concept of vocation which did not include the necessity of a manifestation of special divine predilection for licit entry into the religious life.

On the positive side, the Greek Fathers, Saints Basil, (23) Gregory Nazianzen, (24) and John Chrysostom (347-407) (25) may be cited as explicitly teaching that the life of evangelical perfection by divine invitation is open to any and every Christian who wills to embrace it, and the Latin Fathers are seen to be no less firm in the same opinion, (26) Saint Augustine being so convinced of its validity that the question of what would happen to the human race if all men accepted Christ's challenge troubled him not at all: it would simply bring about a more speedy completion of the city of God! (27)

An outstanding exception to this unanimity of opinion, however, is found to be Saint Thomas himself, although he is commonly and erroneously cited by

(22) Brown, *The Invalidating Effects of Force, Fear, and Fraud Upon the Canonical Novitiate*, The Catholic University of America Canon Law Studies, n. 311 (Washington, D. C.: The Catholic University of America Press, 1951), p. 3 (hereafter cited *Religious Impediments*). Father Brown conclusively proves in his patient and scholarly study that this child oblation constituted a valid and final profession which needed no subsequent ratification on the part of the child, when he reached the use of reason, to bind him to the religious state for his entire lifetime. By the offering of his parents he became a true religious. Cf. *op. cit.*, pp. 3-19. The legal recognition of this practice and its effect on the juridic concept of divine vocation shall be considered in the second section of this article.

(23) Ep. 173: "Evangelicum vivendi genus amplecti cujusvis est."—*MPG*, XXXII, 647-649.

(24) *Orat. 37 in S. Matt.*, 19, 11: "Non omnes, inquit, capiunt verbum istud, sed quibus datum est. . . . Cum audieris quibus datum est, adde: vocatis datum est, atque iis, qui ea animi propensione sunt."—*MPG*, XXXVI, 298.

(25) *In S. Matt.*, 19, 11: "Iis enim datum est qui voluerint . . . "—*MPG*, LVIII, 600; cf. also *De Virginitate*, c. 36 (*MPG*, XLIX, 558).

(26) " . . . sed iis datum est qui petierunt, qui voluerunt, qui ut acciperent, laboraverunt." —S. Jerome (340-420), *Comment. in Matt.* 19, 11 (*MPL*, XXVI, 135); cf. also S. Ambrose, *De Viduis*, c. 13 (*MPL*, XVI, 257-260); S. Jerome, *Contra Vigilantium*, n. 15 (*MPL*, XXIII, 351). Of special interest among later writers are Saint Bernard (1091-1153), *Epistolae Ad Abbatem Columbensem:* "Itaque, ut sentio ego, Regula Sancti Benedicti omni homini proponitur, imponitur nulli. Prodest, si devote suscipitur et tenetur; non tamen, si non suscipitur, obest."—*MPL*, CLXXXII, 862; Saint Ignatius Loyola (1491-1556), quoted in Lehmkuhl, *Theologia Moralis* (9 ed., 2 vols., Friburgi Brisgoviae, 1898), I, c. iv, a. 1, p. 309: "Majora utique signa requiri ad statuendum, quod ea sit Dei voluntas, ut quis in eo statu permaneat, in quo satis sit servare praecepta, quam ut viam consiliorum ingrediatur; quia Dominus tam aperte ad consilia exhortatus sit."

(27) Cf. *De Bono Conjugali*, c. 10—*MPL*, XL, 381. Messenger (*Two in One Flesh*, Vol. I, pp. 10-11) interestingly cites Father Mersch, S.J. (1890-1940) and Tolstoi (1828-1910), both writers of the modern era, as taking the same view, that is, "that such an end to mankind's existence on earth would indeed be 'magnificent', and 'from the supernatural point of view, the most intelligible consummation.' "

authors as favoring the general vocation theory. (28) But while the Angelic Doctor indeed taught that Christ issued an external invitation to *all men* to follow the way of the counsels, (29) he did not permit anyone to follow this general, external call unless he had at the same time an internal vocation, a special and particular grace, which God in His Providence gives to some men and not to others, that these predestined individuals might have the convcition of mind and affection of will which will efficaciously result in the "*propositum religionis assumendae.*" For St. Thomas, the general call was a true vocation, but only dispositively so: it had no efficacy save that of disposing one's mind by focusing the attention upon Christ's words. To be effective, this universal, external call desperately needed the active help of the particular, internal call, a grace that was not given to all. Father Farrell has made a valuable contribution in bringing the true doctrine of Saint Thomas clearly to light, showing that it not only follows necessarily from his general teaching on grace and predestination, but is also found explicitly stated in his treatment of religious vocation. (30)

The theory of a general vocation to the religious state, however, appears to have enjoyed a common acceptance until the seventeenth century. Indeed, there was such a practical application of this broad opinion of religious vocation, that grave abuses in the admitting of candidates brought about a regrettable lowering of religious discipline. It was in order to counteract these abuses that many theologians and spiritual writers began emphasizing the need for a special call from God before one could licitly embrace the religious state (or the priesthood), the requirements being exaggerated to such a point in the eighteenth and nineteenth centuries that vocation came to be considered a *positive impulse*, an *attraction* or intimate message from God, which could not be ignored without sin, and which was considered by some to be so imperious that even ecclesiastical authority could not rightly refuse a candidate so chosen by God. (31) In the year 1909 Canon Joseph Lahitton, of the Diocese of Aire in France, in his celebrated *La Vocation Sacerdotale*, not only dealt a death blow to the unwarranted

(28) Cf. Vermeersch, *De Religiosis Institutis et Personis* (2 vols., Vol. II, 3 ed., Brugis, 1909), pp. 36 ff., an English translation of the tract on vocation being contained in Vermeersch, *Religious and Ecclesiastical Vocation* (translation by J. G. Kempf, St. Louis: B. Herder, 1925), pp. 26 ff.; Coronata, *Institutiones*, I, 703, n. 564; Schaefer, *De Religiosis*, p. 410; Bakalarczyk, *De Novitiatu*, The Catholic University of America Canon Law Studies, n. 36 (Washington, D. C.: The Catholic University of America, 1927), p. 82; Prümmer, *Manuale*, q. 200; Piat, *Compendium Praelectionum Iuris Regularis* (edited by Victorius ab Appeltern, Parisiis-Tornaci, 1903), p. 21 (hereafter cited *Compendium*).

(29) Cf. *supra*, p. 37.

(30) Cf. Farrell, *Theology of Religious Vocation*, pp. 16, 30-31, 44-47, 74-80, 83-85, and the references to the works of Saint Thomas there cited.

(31) For a critical appraisal of the attraction theory and a listing of the many authors who espoused it in one form or another, cf. Farrell, *op. cit.*, pp. 10-19.

exaggerations of this theory, (32) but, as has been seen, (33) opposed *any* internal vocation concept as being too subtle and impracticable, and placed the *totality* of a religious vocation in its strict sense (as well as a vocation to the priesthood) in the call of a legitimate ecclesiastical superior, his thesis subsequently finding favor with many.

Today much doubt and confusion still persists in the speculative domain about the precise nature of the call which is the very essence of God's invitation to the religious state. Besides those who follow Lahitton's view, some authors emphasize the general external invitation of the Scriptures as constituting a sufficient notion of divine vocation, and there are others who make a special point of that which Lahitton discarded as too subtle and useless and propose the *general internal* vocation theory, teaching that the graces involved in religious vocation are the same graces given to all men which happen to be rendered efficacious in a particular instance by the free consent of man. (34) Then there are those authors who insist upon the reality and the necessity for a special internal grace, by which only, for them, is religious vocation constituted, interpreting the Fathers in the light of espoused theological opinions and citing their authority only as regards the existence and not the efficacy of the external divine call. Father Farrell, who in his excellent work has shown himself to be an outstanding proponent of the last named theory, has correctly observed that one's concept of religious vocation will largely be determined by one's acceptance of one or the other theory on grace, predestination and free will, a Thomist, for example, being forced logically to embrace the special internal vocation concept, (35) and Suarez's doctrine on these controversial

(32) The important legal repercussions which this book produced will be considered in the following section of this article. It may be mentioned here, however, that while Lahitton's work is primarily concerned with vocation to the priesthood, it has, *a fortiori*, an application to the religious life and, moreover, the author explicitly states that he intends much of his work to be applied to religious vocation. Cf. *op. cit.*, *Preface* and pp. 253-255.

(33) *Supra*, p. 36.

(34) Farrell, *op. cit.*, examines Lahitton's view on pages 17-28, the general external vocation theory on pages 28-31, and the concept of a general internal vocation on pages 31-36.

(35) Some authors, however, have not shown themselves to be so consistent. Carr, for example, in his work *Vocation to the Priesthood*, states in a footnote on page 56 that, while he does not wish to enter into the controversy whether there is truly a special divine vocation to the religious state, he holds to the negative opinion. And yet in chapter II of the same work he invokes the Thomistic doctrine to explain the nature and activity of the efficacious vocational grace to the priesthood (cf. *op. cit.*, pp. 11-15). One cannot adhere to the Thomistic theory in one instance and not in the other and still be logical. It would be interesting to know if all of the other canonists who shall be seen to profess the general religious vocation theory are, as dogmatic theologians, opposed to the Thomistic theory of grace. Once again Yelle's observation is pertinent: "The institutions of canon law teach the positive determinations which have been adopted from dogmatic and moral theology."—*loc. cit.*

subjects being the backbone of the general internal vocation concept. (36)

Since it is not the purpose of this study, however, to attempt a solution of this highly controversial matter, the writer does not deem it expedient here even to make known his preference for one or the other theory. (37) But what is pertinent to the end of this work is an accurate statement of the problem as it very much exists and with which the legislator is confronted, as he attempts both to obey in full the Divine Will and to give to individuals the freedom which should rightfully be theirs when they seek to follow the way of perfection. Such a statement, it is hoped, is sufficiently contained in the synopsis of the preceding pages, so that with a realization regarding the magnitude and the seriousness of the task before the legislator, one may now confidently look to the vast body of ecclesiastical legislation for a safe guide and norm of action, whereby both truth is protected and serious practical errors and injurious extremes are avoided. (38)

2. Divine religious vocation and ecclesiastical legislation.

By an authoritative declaration of the Holy See in the year 1912, it is now certain that no extraordinary illuminating and impelling graces need to be given by God to those who are called to the religious state; no supernatural mystical attraction, strong and permanent inclination, or sweet impulse felt in the profound depths of the soul making the recipient certain that God is calling

(36) Farrell, *op. cit.*, pp. 34-35. It should be observed that while a Thomist must logically hold to the special divine vocation concept, one who accepts the theories of Molina (1535-1600) and the Congruists on grace could, by a certain adaptation, espouse either a general or special concept of vocation and still be consistent, but more likely would be inclined to the former. For an excellent exposition of the various systems on grace, predestination and free will, cf. Garrigou-Lagrange-Rose, *The One God* (St. Louis: Herder, 1944). It is to be kept in mind, however, that since the work is an apologia for the Thomistic position it will be highly critical of the other theories. Cf. also Hervé, *Manuale Theologiae Dogmaticae* (4 vols., Vol. III, 18, ed., Westminster, Md.: Newman, 1943), Vol. III, nn. 108-122, pp. 128-143.

(37) Because the Church has not definitively declared how the doctrine of efficacious grace is to be reconciled with human liberty, one may follow his choice of many proposed systems, and consequently may espouse either the general or the special divine vocation theory. Cf. Hervé, *op. cit.*, Vol. III, n. 122, p. 143. But cf. also the strict admonition of Pope Paul V (1605-1621): "Vetitum est, in questione hac pertractranda ne quis partem suae oppositam aut qualificaret aut censura quapiam notaret . . . Quin optat etiam [Pontifex], ut verbis asperioribus amaritiem animi significantibus invicem abstineant."—Denzinger-Bannwart-Umberg, *Enchiridion Symbolorum, Definitionum et Declarationum de Rebus Fidei et Morum* (21.-23. ed., Friburgi Brisgoviae, 1932), n. 1090 (hereafter cited *Enchiridion*).

(38) To note a similar instance wherein the law of the Church gives a practical norm of action in the face of a theoretical controversy might be helpful. It is to be recalled that while it is the common opinion today that the human soul is infused into the body at the moment of conception, this opinion is as yet neither philosophically certain nor scientifically demonstrated, and as is fairly generally known, Saint Thomas held that the infusion of the soul did not take place until sometime after conception. Cf. Phillips, *Modern Thomistic Philosophy* (2 vols., Westminster, Md.: Newman, 1934), pp. 312-316; Vacant, Mangenot, Amann,

him, is necessary, or even ordinarily present, in a religious vocation. (39) For Canon Lahitton's aforementioned treatise on the priesthood had stirred up the vocation controversy to a degree so acute, that Pope Pius X appointed a special commission of Cardinals to examine the work, and on July 1st, 1912, its findings were officially pronounced in a letter to the Bishop of Aire from Cardinal Merry del Val, Secretary of State to Pope Pius. (40) The decision declared that the work of Canon Lahitton was in no way to be condemned, and officially approved it in these three specific points: 1) no one has any right to ordination antecedent to the call of the bishop; 2) a positive impulse of the Holy Spirit, or an internal attraction of the subject, is not requisite for a sacerdotal vocation, nor is it ordinarily given; 3) on the contrary, in order to be rightly called by the bishop, the candidate needs nothing further than the right intention and fitness to fulfill the duties of the priesthood properly. (41)

Applying this decree of 1912, with obvious reservations and distinctions, to religious vocation, (42) it is therefore certain that the tenets of the attraction theory are no longer to be used as valid norms of judgment in any attempt to discern the presence or the absence of a call to the religious state, and neither

---

Dictionnaire de Théologie Catholique (30 vols., incomplete, Vol. I, 3. ed., Paris: Letouzey et Ane, 1930), s.v. "*ame*," Vol. I, cols., 1028 ff. But while either view might be held theoretically, therefore, whenever there is a question of a soul's eternal salvation, the Church demands that every living human fetus, no matter what its stage of development, be considered as possessing a human soul and be baptized absolutely. Cf. can. 747. One may here well note that the legislator not only gives a practical norm of action, but by his use of the word "absolutely" indicates his adherence to a definite opinion, the one which holds to the infusion of the soul at the moment of conception. One may well look for similar indication of opinion in the question of religious vocation.

(39) This is not to deny the possibility of a *very special* vocation being given in rare instances. It would be rash to discredit entirely, or to deride the possibility of, the manifestation of God's Will in this manner, for to eliminate it would amount to placing a limit on divine action. Indeed, as is well known, history is not without examples of such special acts of divine providence.

(40) *AAS*, IV (1912), 485. The following year Cardinal Merry del Val wrote to Canon Lahitton himself informing him that Pope Pius X had fully approved the decisions of the Commission. Cf. *AAS*, V (1913), 290.

(41) As some authors have correctly interpreted the decree, the decision of the Commission was not an endorsement of the canon's own thesis that the *totality* of priestly vocation consists in the bishop's call. Cf. Farrell, *Theology of Religious Vocation*, p. 19: "But the decree is not a blanket endorsement of the whole book, *La Vocation Sacerdotale*. Rather the terms of the decisions state that this work is worthy of praise so far as it contains the three propositions singled out and formulated by the Commission, which for the most part embody the negative portion of Canon Lahitton's thesis. His positive teaching stands and falls on its own merits and defects." Cf. also Duffy, *Testing The Spirit* (St. Louis: B. Herder, 1948), pp. 151-154.

(42) Cf. Duffy, *op. cit.*, pp. 147-151, for a detailed application. It should be observed, however, that Father Duffy espouses the special divine vocation theory (cf. p. 154) and his application will necessarily be influenced thereby.

the candidate nor the admitting superior need pay them any heed. While this undoubtedly is universally understood by religious superiors, it is a matter of rather common experience that it is not so well understood by many young men and women who are inclined to the life of perfection, but hesitate to embrace it because of false notions about the nature of vocation. Pastors, confessors, superiors and others who have to do with the guidance of souls in the matter of vocation to the religious life, and who have been asked by the present Holy Father to promote such holy vocations, (43) should therefore see to it that the decree of 1912 is made known and understood by their charges.

But while the decision of the Holy See gave the "coup de grâce" to a false exaggeration which had held almost undisputed sway for nigh onto three centuries, it by no means settled the fundamental controversy on religious vocation, namely, whether it be a special or a general divine call. For an indication of the legislator's mind on this matter and a practical norm of action, other canonical sources must be resorted to.

a. Pre-Code legislation and divine religious vocation.

A partial survey of the pre-Code legislation relative to the admission of candidates into the religious state and an eclectic presentation of the matter could undoubtedly do much to convince the uninitiated that the juridic concept of religious vocation *certainly* excluded the necessity of a special divine call, by which some men only are selected for the religious state in preference to others. Adding particular emphasis to this conviction would be the legislator's long recognition of the custom, referred to above, (44) of parents offering their infant children into the monastic life and binding them there absolutely and perpetually, *the children becoming true religious by this parental oblation*. For it cannot be doubted, as Brown has demonstrated, that while occasional attempts were made, both in and out of the councils of the West, to require a subsequent ratification on the part of the "*pueri oblati*" when they had reached the use of reason, (45) the Benedictine concept of the institute, which viewed a parent's offering of his child as having all the juridical effects of any valid and final profession without the need for a subsequent ratification, (46) quite generally pre-

(43) Cf. Pius XII, motu propr. *De institutorum saecularium laude atque confirmatione*, 12 martr. 1948—*AAS*, XL (1948), 286.

(44) Cf. *supra*, pp. 38-39.

(45) This was the practice in the monasteries of Saint Basil, for although Basilian monasticism introduced the custom of the acceptance of child oblates into the religious life, this Holy Founder did not regard the practice as setting up an absolute and perpetual bond between the child and the monastery, but stated in his Rule that these children were not to make their final profession until they had reached an age when they were capable of acting with full knowledge and liberty. Cf. Brown, *Religious Impediments*, pp. 5-6; *Reg. fus. tract.*, X—*MPG*, XXXI, 951, 955.

(46) Brown, *op. cit.*, pp. 6-8; cf. also Deroux, *Les Origines de l'Oblature Bénédictine* (Vienne, 1927), p. 13; Delatte, *Commentary on the Rule of St. Benedict* (New York: Benziger, 1921), p. 407.

vailed in ecclesiastical legislation until late in the twelfth century, the canons reproducing and crystallizing that concept. (47) The attempts of the glossators on the *Decree* of Gratian (48) to bring this ancient law on the oblation into conformity with the new general legislation of the twelfth and thirteenth centuries, which obliterated all the juridical binding force that had been attached to the custom of child oblation, do not reflect the true interpretation of the former laws in their original sense, and the glosses read meanings into them which clearly they never had when they were formulated. (49)

The proponents of the general divine vocation theory, therefore, have here a telling argument. For if licit entry into the religious state depends upon the special predilection of Divine Providence, granting the grace of vocation to some and not to others, how then is this legal sanction of a practice which seems diametrically opposed to such a concept to be explained, a sanction, it is to be noted, which was as long-lived as it was wide-spread? These children were offered and *perpetually bound* to the religious state before it was in any way physically or morally possible to determine signs of God's predilection in the matter, an infant, of course, being radically incapable of forming a "*propositum religionis assumendae*," and unless the legislator believed that the grace to do so *would* be given him when he attained the use of reason, so that he could make the meritorious "*propositum*" if he but willed to, how could that legislator possibly justify himself in forcing him, and under the most severe penalties, (50) to remain a religious the rest of his life? In other words, it may be argued, the practice of the Church cannot otherwise be explained or justified unless it is admitted that *all men* have, or at least are able to have if they will, the grace efficaciously to embrace the religious state, which is the same thing as saying that a special divine vocation is not necessary to enter that life licitly. (51)

(47) Cf. Brown, *op. cit.*, pp. 8-19, and the references to pertinent legislation there cited. It is to be noted that the institute was not only recognized in particular conciliar law, but that various Popes also considered the oblate profession as constituting one a true religious for life.

(48) Gratian incorporated a good many of the ancient canons in such a way so as to substantiate his own approval of the institute. Cf. the *dictum* before c. 2, C. XX, q. 1; the *dicta* after c. 1, C. XX, q. 1, and c. 7, C. XX, q. 1; and cc. 2, 3, 4, 5, 6, C. XX, q. 1.

(49) Cf. Brown, *op. cit.*, p. 18.

(50) Neither the child oblate nor the professed adult, because they were both professed religious, were ever permitted to leave the monastery. This prohibition was binding under the pain of excommunication. Cf. Brown, *op. cit.*, pp. 9-10.

(51) This is not in any way to defend the grave abuse of "forced vocations," a practice which not only indefensibly encumbers a person with a tremendous burden, but, as can be easily understood, may actually endanger his eternal salvation by imposing upon him a state for which he has neither the suitability nor the interest. Canon 2352 inflicts an automatic excommunication upon anyone who in any way compels either a man or a woman to enter a religious institute or to make a religious profession therein. But what is stressed by the argument is that past canonical recognition of the practice of "child oblation" seems to

The argument, thus formulated, has definite cogency, nor has it been overlooked by advocates of the general divine vocation theory. (52) And adding further weight to this line of reasoning is the fact that, contrary to the established custom in the religious life, infants could never lawfully be offered for Sacred Orders, (53) while at the same time canonical sources, early and late, reveal a marked emphasis placed by the legislator on the need for special divine predilection antecedent to licit priestly ordination. (54) But legal recognition of the practice of child oblation is not the only possible indication of the legislator's mind on the subject of divine religious vocation, and a more complete and critical examination of pertinent texts is in order. (55)

As shall be demonstrated in the following chapter, it has always been a matter of the utmost concern to the legislator that only fit and worthy candidates be admitted to the religious state. Especially pertinent to the subject at hand, however, is his unremitting insistence through history that applicants give evidence of their suitability by having a right intention, an intention which, as has been seen, can be formed only under the influence of divine grace. (56) Only those candidates are to be allowed to make religious profession who, when truly

---

indicate the legislator's conviction that, despite any such burden imposed upon the individual, the grace of vocation is present for him to use, *and he is capable*, even though with difficulty, of making the efficacious will act to utilize it.

(52) Cf. Piat-Victorius ab Appeltern, *Compendium*, p. 22, q. 28; Beste, *Introductio*, pp. 361-362; Prümmer, *Manuale*, p. 268, q. 200.

(53) Carr, *Vocation to the Priesthood*, p. 56, note 13.

(54) There can be no misconstruing the legislator's mind on this latter matter, for too often he has placed the basic requirement of a special God-given summons to Sacred Orders in sharp relief: one may not enter the priesthood simply at his own will, but only as a consequence of having been singled out by divine activity in the order of grace; bishops are accountable to God should they elevate to the priestly dignity someone of whose divine vocation they are in doubt, that is, when there is no positive evidence that a divine call has been given; no one can be God's minister unless elected by God, his ordination must be the consequence of divine judgment, etc. Cf. Carr, *op. cit.*, pp. 16-29, for a textual demonstration of this matter. But while he invokes the Thomistic theory on grace to explain this divine predilection (cf. pp. 11-15), it should be noted that the doctrine of the special call to the priesthood is not to be held in irreconcilable opposition to the other theories on grace which, of course, admit the existence of truly efficacious grace, as indeed all acceptable theories must. Cf. Hervé, *op. cit.*, III, pp. 124-128.

(55) The writer does not pretend that in what follows he has completely exhausted all the legislator has to say concerning the divine call to the religious life; but in view of the relative paucity of canonical texts on divine religious vocation, he believes that the presentation is comprehensive enough to be truly indicative of the state of affairs as it existed before the Code of Canon Law.

(56) Cf. *supra*, pp. 34-36.

and sincerely (57) moved by divine love, (58) hasten to the service of God, (59) desiring to imitate Him in humility and obedience and to progress in the virtues, (60) their intention being truly supernatural, (61) and not colored by any ulterior designs of material interest, provision for life, honor or dignities. (62)

But while the role of divine grace, necessarily implied in the texts concerning right intention, has thus been always given full recognition, both in particular and general legislation on admission to the religious state, these texts do not of themselves solve the problem whether the necessary grace is made available to all or to just a selected few. Indeed the texts can be utilized to serve either side of the controversy without any evident distortion of the meaning of words. The advocates of the general vocation theory, for example, will say that the supernatural motive the legislator demands for one to embrace the religious life licitly is the result of man's cooperation with a grace which is denied to no one, while those of the opposite opinion will hold that the "*propositum religionis*" is the efficacious result of a special grace of divine predilection, both sides readily agreeing that the "right intention" by all means must be present for a licit religious profession. It is when these texts are viewed in conjunction with certain others, however, that a more impressive argument can be formulated—and yet even here an ecletic presentation of material may very well make the legislator seem to espouse two widely divergent views.

The proponents of the general vocation theory, for example, relying firmly on their argument of the legal recognition of child oblation, can further point to the fact that when the legislator speaks of the note of "selection" contained in the concept of religious profession, as far as God and man are concerned, the emphasis often is placed on "the individual choosing God" rather than on "God choosing the individual." Many such instances can be shown. When the Council of Chalcedon forbade monks to enter the military life or to seek worldly dignities, and excommunicated religious of either sex who married, the reason given

(57) IV Council of Chalcedon (451), can. 4: "Qui vere et sincere monasticam vitam aggrediuntur, digne convenienti honore habeantur."—Mansi, VII, 359; cf. Codex Iuris Canonici, c. 487.

(58) S. Gregory I (590-604), decr., 5 iul. 595, cap. VI: " . . . qui divino amore districtiorem appetit subire servitutem."—Mansi, X, 436.

(59) *Loc. cit.*

(60) Cf. S. Sergius I (687-701), epist. *Ea quae* (anno circiter 688)—*Bull. Rom. Taur.*, I, 212.

(61) "Probate spiritus, si ex Deo sunt." Cf. Gregory IX (1227-1241), epist. decret. *Non solum*, 13 iul. 1236—*Collectanea Sacrae Congregationis de Religiosis*, *Enchiridion de Statibus Perfectionis* (Vol. I, *Documenta Ecclesiae Sodalibus Instituendis*, Romae: Officium Libri Catholici, (1949), p. 30 (hereafter cited S. C. de Religiosis, *Enchiridion*); Clement VIII (1592-1605), const. *Cum ad regularem*, 19 mart. 1603, §2—*Fontes*, n. 189; S.C. super Statu Regularium, decr. *Ad propagandam*, 1 ian. 1658—S. C. de Religiosis, *Enchiridion*, p. 121.

(62) Council of Rome (1059), c. VII—*Bull. Rom. Taur.*, I, 661; I Provincial Council of Cologne (1536), decr. X, c. IV—Mansi, XXXII, 1278-1282.

was that *they had already chosen God* and dedicated themselves to Him, no mention being made of God having selected them for higher things. (63) Pope Saint Gregory I, in insisting on the testimony of good character which candidates for the monastic life must present, made no reference to such as being evidence of God's predilection, but emphasized rather the candidates' desire to enter the service of God. (64) The Trullan Council in 692 thought of every Christian as being able to choose the monastic life, (65) but once having assumed the Lord's cross in religious profession it was not permitted a Christian to cast it aside, (66) for a spiritual man does not change his good purpose. (67) And thus, in a more or less similar vein, does a vast amount of legislation on the religious life seem to indicate the legislator's preoccupation with the individual's choice of God rather than God's choice of the individual.

On the other hand, however, a careful investigation of the legal literature relative to the religious state not only reveals several texts which seem better understood in the light of the special divine vocation theory, but some indeed which on the surface appear definitely misleading apart from it. Pope Urban II (1088-1099), (68) for example, in being asked what the law was concerning secular clerics who wished to enter a monastery against their bishop's wishes, replied that the private law written in the heart of man through the inspiration of the Holy Spirit had to be considered, and therefore *whoever was led by the Holy Spirit*, even though his bishop opposed him, should not be constrained by public law from embracing the monastic life, for the private law of the spirit is of greater dignity than the public law. (69) Here indeed, it seems, is specific recognition

(63) Cc. VII, XVI—Mansi, VII, 375, 377-378.

(64) Decr., 5 iul. 595, cap. VI—Mansi, X, 436.

(65) C. XLIII: "Licet omni christiano vitam exerciatricem eligere, et rerum ad vitam pertinentium deposita tempestate, monasterium ingredi, et habitu monachi tonderi, in quacumque prolapsione deprehensus fuerit."—Mansi, XI, 963.

(66) Cf. Anastasius IV (1153-1154), epist. decret. *Christianae fidei*, 21 oct. 1154—*Bull. Rom. Taur.*, II, 620.

(67) Cf. Alexander III (1159-1181), epist. decret.—c. 4, X, *de voto et voti redemptione*, III, 34.

(68) It is of importance as well as of interest to note that the texts which follow are comparatively late as regards the time of their origin, the more explicit of them corresponding to the period in which the necessity of a special divine call was all but unanimously held by theologians and spiritual writers (cf. *supra*, p. 40). It is quite possible, of course, that the legislator was greatly influenced by this theological opinion in the phrasing of his laws.

(69) Duae sunt . . . leges: una publica, altera privata. Publica. . . . Lex vero privata est quae instinctu Sancti Spiritus in corde scribitur, sicut de quibusdam dicit Apostolus: "Qui habeant legem Dei scriptam in cordibus suis." . . . Si quis horum in ecclesia sua sub episcopo populum retinet, et seculariter vivit, si afflatus Spiritu Sancto in aliquo monasterio vel regulari canonica salvare se voluerit, quia lege privata ducitur, nulla ratio exigit, ut a publica lege constringatur. Dignior est enim lex privata quam publica. Spiritus quidem Dei lex est, et qui Spiritu Dei aguntur lege Dei ducuntur; et quis est, qui possit Sancto Spiritui digne re-

of the special grace of religious vocation, and a recognition which does not appear to consider this special grace too extraordinary an occurrence, for the Pontiff's reply is in the form of a general answer to a general problem. The *glossa ordinaria*, moreover, in commenting on this answer of Pope Urban and raising several objections which the entrance of a secular cleric into the religious state seemed to present, unraveled these difficulties by a very short and simple solution: a cleric was free to leave his charge to enter the religious life because he acted according to the inspiration of the Holy Spirit. (70) Pope Innocent III (1198-1216), in a letter dated April 29, 1206, referred to this letter of Pope Urban and adopted its line of reasoning when dealing with the problem of the transfer of a professed religious of one institute to an institute of stricter life: the public law of the Church which forbade such a transfer did not apply to those individuals who acted with humility and purity of heart, *for they were led by the Holy Spirit* and possessed freedom under the private law. (71) But while these texts point to the existence of a special divine call to the religious life in at least certain instances, they do not necessarily imply that such a call need always be present for licit religious profession. In other words, the texts do not of themselves preclude the possibility that man might reason efficaciously to the desirability of the evangelical counsels and licitly enter the religious state, by cooperating with a grace which is common to all men.

Certain other texts, however, do not so readily lend themselves to such an explanation, and a mere statement of them presents a weighty argument to the effect that the legislator held that a special call from God is a necessary prerequisite for licit entry into the religious state. The Provincial Council of Bordeaux (1583), for instance, stated that it was aware of the danger to religious discipline deriving from the admission of candidates who had not been called by the Holy Spirit, and therefore ordered superiors to seek positive signs of divine vocation in a candidate, even though such a requirement might lessen the number of religious:

Et quia experientia docet, disciplinam religiosam, eorum vitio ex parte collapsam esse, qui in religiosas familias intrusi, aut alia quavis ratione humana inducti potius, quam a

---

sistere? Quisquis igitur hoc Spiritu ducitur, etiam episcopo contradicente, eat liber nostra auctoritate. Iusto enim lex non est posita, sed ubi Spiritus Dei, ibi libertas, et si Spiritu Dei ducimini, non estis sub lege."—c. 2, C. XIX, q. 2; JE, n. 5760.

(70) *Glossa ordinaria* ad c. 2, C. XIX, q. 2, s.v. *Si afflatus:* " . . . excusatur a delicto instinctu Spiritu Sancto." St. Thomas Aquinas repeated this canon of Gratian (c. 2, C. XIX, q. 2) in his *Summa Theologica* (IIa, IIae, q. 189, a. 7) and agreed with its reasoning. Cf. also S. C. Ep. et Reg., resolutio *Pinerolien.*, 28 iul. 1837—*Fontes*, n. 1914; S. C. Ep. et. Reg., resolutio, *Aurelianen.*, 20 dec. 1859—*Fontes*, n. 1979.

(71) C. 18 (licet), X, *de regularibus et transeuntibus ad religionem*, III, 31; Potthast, *Regesta Pontificum Romanorum inde ab anno post Christum* natum 1198 ad annum 1304 (2 vols., Berolini, 1874-1875), n. 2763 (hereafter cited Potthast). Cf. the *glossa ordinaria* to this canon, s.v. *licentiam postulaverit:* "Sed illius auctoritate canonis fit instinctu Spiritus Sancti, et ita non constringitur per legem;" and s.v. *ex lege privata.*

sancto Spiritu vocati fuerunt; diligentissime superiores animum atque voluntatem eorum explorent, qui ad novitiatum vel professionem admittendi erunt, nec quemquam recipiant, aut profiteri nullo modo permittant, nisi de divina eius vocatione, atque etiam perseverandi voluntate non obscura sed perspicua argumenta habuerint, licet pauciores futuri sint religiosi. (72)

Pope Clement VIII (1592-1605) in his constitution *Cum ad regularem*, after commanding superiors to inquire diligently into the motives which prompted aspirants to ask for acceptance into the religious state, (73) instructed novice masters to see that their charges understood the excellence of the "divine vocation of which they had been made worthy." (74) Pope Alexander VII (1655-1677) in the year 1658 declared that neophytes as such (*per se*) were not to be excluded from the religious state, but that all who "are moved by the spirit of God and strive after perfection" are to be received. (75) The Sacred Congregation on the Discipline of Regulars in the year 1695 reminded religious that *under divine inspiration* they had renounced worldly desires and *had been called* to follow the footsteps of their Saviour, (76) and the Sacred Congregation *super Statu Regularium* in a decree issued on January 25, 1848, ordered that for the religious state there were to be received only those candidates who, "led by a sublime call," (77) have been proven to be "truly suitable according to the will of God." (78)

But especially after the middle of the nineteenth century did the legislator show himself to be most concerned with the presence of a divine vocation in those seeking admission to the religious state. Pope Pius IX (1846-1878) on several occasions demanded that aspirants give "signs of a true vocation," (79)

---

(72) C. XXV—Mansi, XXXIV, 779.

(73) Const. *Cum ad regularem*, 19 mart. 1603, n. 5—*Fontes*, n. 189.

(74) *Ibidem*, §9: "Curam adhibeat diligentem, ut novitii omnes in regulari disciplina sedulo exerceantur, agnoscantque praecipue divinae, qua digni facti sunt, vocationis praestantiam, et excellentiam, quae vera sit, atque perfecta votorum solemnium, et quam necessaria suisque Ordinis Constitutionum observantia. . . . "

(75) Const. *Sacrosancti*, 18 ian. 1658, §2, n. VI: "Neophytos Deo sub Religionis iugo servire volentes sine rationabili causa regulares non respuant, sed pari charitate omnes, qui spiritu Dei aguntur, et ad perfectionem anhelant, amplectantur."—*Fontes*, n. 235.

(76) Decr. *Sanctissimus*, 18 iul. 1695: "Nimis enim turpe esset, eos ad saecularia desideria, quibus semel, aspirante Domino, renunciarunt, animum revocare. . . . Meminerint se ad peculiarem Salvatoris Nostri sequelam vocatos. . . . "—S. C. de Religiosis, *Enchiridion*, p. 132.

(77) Decr. *Regulari disciplinae*, 25 ian. 1845, preamble—*Fontes*, n. 4376.

(78) *Loc. cit.* Cf. also *ibidem*, *pars secunda*, n. IV: "Magister novitiorum referat de novitii agendi ratione in novitiatu servata de eius libertate, vocatione et idoneitate ad statum religiosum."

(79) Ep. *Nostis et Nobiscum*, 8 dec. 1849, n. 26: "(Moderatores) illos tantum ad religiosam professionem admittant, qui tyrocinio rite posito ea dederint verae vocationis signa . . . "—*Fontes*, n. 508; litt. ap. *Ad universalis Ecclesiae*, 7 febr. 1862: "ne quis admittatur, qui saeculi contagione pollutus electum Christi gregem inficiat; vel verae vocationis expers, susceptique

and particularly explicit on this matter were many decrees of councils (the Vatican Council [1869-1870] as well as several provincial councils) and of the Sacred Congregations enacted during his reign. The provincial council of Bourges (1850), for example, in an admonition to directors of souls and to parents, ordered that "they use the greatest prudence in the matter of determining the vocation of youths, lest perhaps, with the gravest danger to salvation, those who are called decline to enter the religious state or there presume to enter it those who have not been called." (80) Similarly the provincial synod of Utrecht (1865) cautioned against admitting those who "are not led by a divine vocation," (81) as did the Sacred Congregation *super Statu Regularium*, (82) and in the schemata of the proposed decrees of the Vatican Council (83) many instances may be indicated which show concern that evidences of a divine vocation be present in candidates before they may be admitted into the religious state. (84) In like manner, the Sacred Congregation of Religious on September 7, 1909, issued a decree which stated that only those who show signs of having received a divine call are to be allowed to follow the evangelical counsels in a religious institute, (85) and this same Congregation in subsequent legislation quite often referred to the divine vocation to the religious life in such a way as to seem to substantiate the views of the proponents of the special vocation theory. (86)

Instituti pertaesus gravem sodalibus molestiam inferat cum disciplinae perturbatione, et regularis observantiae discrimine."—*Fontes*, n. 532.

(80) Tit. II, decr. *De Congregationibus Religiosis—Collectio Lacensis: Acta et Decreta Sacrorum Conciliorum Recentium* (7 vols., Friburgi-Brisgoviae: Herder, 1870-1892), IV, 1099-1100 (hereafter cited *Coll. Lac.*).

(81) Decreta, tit. VII—Mansi, XLVIII, 771.

(82) Cf. Declaratio super litt. circ. *Neminem latet*, 16 aug. 1866—Bizzarri, *Collectanea*, p. 866.

(83) The Vatican Council did not publish any disciplinary decrees, but in the schemata which were drawn up the mind of the Church is very clearly expressed.

(84) Cf., for example, *Schemata Constitutionum de Regularibus*, n. 6, preamble: " . . . nihil tam est accommodum ac necessarium, quam ut novitii sedulo recteque instituantur, ac vera eorum vocatio ad religiosam vitam serio diligenterque probetur"—S. C. de Religiosis, *Enchiridion*, p. 200; cf. also cap. II and IV—*op. cit.*, pp. 201, 202.

(85) Decr. *Ecclesia Christi*, 7 sept. 1909: "Ecclesia Christi, licet spirituali guadio afficiatur, quum fideles matura deliberatione et recta intentione statum perfectionis in religiosis Familiis amplectuntur, qualitatis tamen quam numeri potius sollicita, ingressum in novitiatum et professionem votorum ita moderata est, ut eos tantum decreverit ad evangelica consilia in religiosis Domibus servanda esse admittendos, qui divinae vocationis argumenta praeberent."—*AAS*, I (1909), 700.

(86) Cf. decr. *Sacrosancta Dei Ecclesia*, 1 ian. 1911: "Ut igitur dignitas votorum, quae etiam Laici solemni ritu promittunt, in laude, qua in Ecclesia merito gaudent, perseveret, et ad sanctum vocationis propositum impensiore cura provehendum . . . "—*Fontes*, 4407; decr. *Inter reliquas*, 1 ian. 1911: "Caveant autem iuvenes militiae servientes, ne sanctae vocationis donum amittant . . . "—*Fontes*, 4408; instructio *Illud saepius*, 18 aug. 1915: " . . . Sanctitas Sua . . . per hanc Sacram Congregationem iis omnibus qui religiosis Sodalitatibus praesunt

At first glance, therefore, it must be admitted that ecclesiastical legislation relative to divine vocation to the religious state does not give too clear a picture of the legislator's mind as to whether this call is special (in the sense of being given to a few only) or general. While particularly in the question of child oblation it would seem more difficult to reconcile the legislator's action with the special vocation theory, the writer would be rather hesitant to point to an ancient practice of the Church as *absolutely* solving a controversy concerning which the Holy See has since explicitly refused to give a definite answer (i.e., the theological controversy on the specific nature of efficacious grace, so intimately linked with the general-special vocation problem). (87) On the other hand, certain texts to be found in ecclesiastical legislation seem to indicate that the legislator leaned more to the special than to the general vocation theory, but again a caution should be observed lest one be too eager to read one's own opinion into texts, the meaning of which might be variously interpreted. In view of this apparently cloudy legislative pattern, therefore, a few pertinent observations are in order.

In the first place, it should be pointed out that, since in the controversy about the nature of grace and predestination the very same texts of Scripture and Tradition are often used to substantiate directly opposed theories, the legislation which has been considered in the preceding pages could undoubtedly be reconciled with either theory of divine vocation *to the satisfaction of its respective adherents.* Secondly, the legislator who has been referred to so constantly is not a single individual living during one particular period of history, but is a composite of a number of personages who at diverse times and places have enjoyed jurisdiction in the Church and who, while giving recognition to the *necessary* conclusions of theology, have been concerned primarily with the discipline and good order of the religious state, leaving speculative problems of theology to the theologians. Nevertheless one does not (and indeed cannot) abstract altogether from one's theological convictions when one acts as a legislator, and it is quite possible that the exact phrasing of much of the legislation viewed in these pages has been the direct or indirect expression of such convictions. Consequently, it is also possible that the authors of this legislation, both particular and general legislation, have at different times held diverse theological views on the matter of the divine call, and have manifested these diverse views in the particular phrasing of their laws, while at the same time *all* the legislation which they have enacted has been for the same end, the assurance that only fit and

---

duo haec animadvertenda proponit, quibus casuum rectorumque tam deplorandorum praecipua causa et origo continentur, scilicet divini afflatus, seu vocationis, tum defectum tum amissionem. . . . Etenim cum admodum exiguus, nostris hisce temporibus, factus sit eorum numerus qui, divino instinctu permoti, Religionem amplecti studeant, . . . illos tantummodo admitti qui, divino impulsi afflatu, Religionem digne ingredi cogitant . . . serio meditantes vocationem qua vocati sunt . . . "—S. C. de Religiosis, *Enchiridion*, pp. 340, 341, 342.

(87) Cf. *supra*, pp. 36-42.

worthy subjects be accepted into the religious life. And thirdly, and most important, it must be recognized that the texts which have been presented in this section as being pertinent to the problem here considered comprise an extremely small portion of all the legislation which has been enacted on the admission of candidates into the religious state. They have been sifted from a vast body of laws which, as shall be seen at some length in the following chapter, have been directed towards the promotion and conservation of the dignity and the usefulness of the juridic religious state, as well as the good of the individual, of the Church, and of society at large. The writer in viewing this legislation as a whole has gained the impression that the legislator has been concerned primarily with *the fact* of a candidate's suitability for the religious state, rather than with the question whether this fitness is the result of a special divine predilection or of his own efficacious cooperation with a grace that is given to all men. In other words, the actual presence of a divine religious vocation seems of paramount importance to the legislator, and while his particular expression of the laws demanding its presence might at times give rise to diverse interpretations concerning its specific nature, that problem, whether it is a special or general call, he appears willing to leave to the theologians to treat "*ex professo*," and seems confident that no matter what be the final solution, it will not be at odds with the laws he has enacted and their purpose. This impression has been further strengthened for the writer by the phrasing of canon 538 of the present Code of Canon Law. (88)

b. Canon 538 and divine religious vocation

Canon 538, the first canon of Title XI, "*De admissione in religionem*," reads as follows:

> Any Catholic who is not debarred by a legitimate impediment, and is prompted by a right intention, and is fit to bear the burdens of the religious life, may be admitted into the religious state. (89)

"In these concise terms," say Bouscaren-Ellis, "the legislator sums up the essential conditions and the sufficient signs of vocation to the religious life,"

(88) The writer wishes to comment in passing that the texts which have been cited in the preceding pages are not to be found in any of the authors who have been consulted on the subject of religious vocation. He finds it surprising that canonists who discuss the special-general vocation problem rely on the Scriptures, the Fathers and the theologians to give force to their particular preference, and, with the exception of a reference to the ancient legal recognition of the institute of the "*pueri oblati*," do not cite any historical canonical text as giving an indication of the legislator's mind on the subject, one way or the other. Admittedly the writer has not read all that has been written on the question of religious vocation, but among the many authors whom he has read he is unable to point to a single instance in which pre-Code legislation has been quoted with reference to the divine call to the religious state.

(89) "In religionem admitti potest quilibet catholicus qui nullo legitimo detineatur impedimento rectaque intentione moveatur, et ad religionis onera ferenda sit idoneus."

(90) and canonists generally use canon 538 as a springboard to a brief discussion of religious vocation, usually admitting preference for either the special or the general vocation theory. Leaving aside for the moment the implications contained in this canon as regards the *ecclesiastical* call to the religious state, (91) the question under present consideration is: What indication does this particular piece of legislation give regarding the legislator's stand on the *divine* call to that state?

Turning first to the writings of modern canonists, it can readily be seen that canonical commentary on canon 538 is not constant. Woywod (1880-1941), for example, did not bring up the question of religious vocation at all, (92) and in the *Commentary* of Bouscaren-Ellis there is found only the statement already quoted, that here we have the essential conditions and sufficient signs of a religious vocation. (93)

Some authors make a twofold division of the four elements contained in the canon and speak of vocation "considered juridically and theologically." Beste, for instance, lists three of the elements, catholicity, immunity from impediments, and aptitude, as belonging to the external forum of the Church and constituting the juridic vocation, about which religious superiors judge, while he speaks of the right and firm intention as pertaining to the divine forum and being a "theological requisite" (*theologice poscitur*). The four elements taken together, the theological as well as the juridical elements, are, so he says, required and sufficient for what may be called a general divine vocation, while the concept of a special vocation has the added note of a "particular supernatural impulse, by which God predestines and impels a few determined individuals in preference to all other men to embrace the religious life, each candidate being made aware of this call through the divine voice (speaking) in his heart, interior motions, illuminations of the mind and a propensity and inclination for the religious state." The general vocation to the religious life was given to all men when Our Lord invited and exhorted everyone to pursue perfection by means of the evangelical counsels, and the theory which maintains that this general call is sufficient for licit entrance into the religious life "seems to be the truer and better opinion and to have been adopted by the Code in this canon." (94)

Cocchi makes the same distinction between the juridical and theological elements of canon 538 and holds that together they are signs of a true vocation, even for the internal forum, but while he lays down the necessity for a divine vocation he merely states the general-special problem without choosing between

(90) *Commentary*, p. 258; cf. also Creusen-Garesché-Ellis, *Religious Men and Women in the Code*, n. 170, p. 129.

(91) This is the subject matter of the following chapter.

(92) Cf. *Commentary*, I, 240-241.

(93) *Loc. cit.*

(94) Cf. *Introductio*, p. 361.

the two theories. The judgment about the required intention, he says, is made by the one seeking admission; the judgment on the presence in the candidate of the other requisites is made by the admitting superiors with the help of authentic documents. (95)

Schaefer (d.1948) likewise distinguished between the two vocations mentioned in the requirements of this canon: juridically a vocation to the religious life is had if the elements of catholicity, immunity from impediments, and suitability of mind and body are present, for these are external signs concerning which superiors definitively judge in the external forum; a true or divine vocation (*ut dicunt, divinam vocationem*) requires, in addition to these qualities, a right intention, a firm will of perseverance, *and a call on the part of a competent superior*. (96) This substantially was also the doctrine of Vermeersch (1858-1936) who, while allowing for the fact of a divine vocation, in practice identified it with the ecclesiastical call extended by the authorities of the Church when they admit a candidate to religious profession. (97)

Coronata similarly views religious vocation from a twofold aspect, juridic and moral, but he considers the element of right intention, together with the other three, as part of the *juridic question*, although he says that the juridic question "prescinds entirely from any merely internal motions of the soul" (!). (98) The special-general vocation problem is proposed as a moral question, and he thinks that the Code does not wish to offer a solution to the controversy, but instead holds the middle road between the two opinions by requiring the internal (!) element of right intention (99) in addition to certain external qualities,

---

(95) *Commentarium in Codicem Iuris Canonici* (8 vols. in 5, Vol. IV, 3, ed., Taurini: Marietti, 1933), IV, 128-131 (hereafter cited *Commentarium*). Ramstein also leaves the judgment on the presence of a right intention "to the conscience of the individual assisted by the advice of his confessor," and says that it belongs to the religious superiors to determine the presence in the individual candidate of the other conditions. Cf. *A Manual of Canon Law* (Hoboken, N. J.: Terminal Printing and Publishing Co., 1948), p. 330 (hereafter cited *Manual*).

(96) *De Religiosis*, pp. 408-409.

(97) Vermeersch wrote an entire treatise on the subject as early as the year 1903 in which he performed the task of crystallizing the theory of general vocation and putting it in clear and comprehensive terms against the attraction theory. His argument for his thesis is based particularly on the teaching of Scripture, of the Fathers and of the theologians of the middle ages. The treatise may be found in his *De Religiosis Institutis et Personis*, pp. 24-61, and is available also in an English translation by Joseph G. Kempf under the title *Religious and Ecclesiastical Vocation* (St. Louis: B. Herder, 1925).

(98) *Institutiones*, I, 702.

(99) A right intention is, of course, something internal, but as the author has already noted, comes also under the juridic aspect of vocation, and therefore his statement that a juridic vocation "prescinds entirely from any merely internal motions of the soul" can be misleading.

but maintaining an indifferent attitude on whether this is the result of a special or a general divine call. (100)

Regatillo concurs with Coronata in placing a right intention among the elements of a juridic vocation, which vocation, at least, he says, one must have to enter the religious state licitly. He then makes mention of the general-special vocation controversy without showing preference for either opinion, but in his discussion of the question he shows that he considers the general and the juridic vocation to be one and the same thing, and he equates the notion of special vocation with the note of an internal call. (101)

Prümmer (1866-1931) regarded the general divine vocation theory as the truer and better doctrine, because "the Code of Canon Law in enumerating the requisite condition for admission into the religious state speaks indeed of a right intention, but maintains a deep silence about a divine vocation; which clearly indicates that a special divine vocation is not required. On the other hand, it supposes a special divine vocation for the clerical state, as is apparent from canon 1353." (102)

Augustine was more cautious in stating his opinion on the question, for he explained that "it is not without reason . . . that canonists require a special vocation as a condition of admission to the religious state . . . (and) the word of our Lord: 'He that can take it, let him take it,' (Matt. 19, 12) is a strong argument in favor of a special vocation, unless we choose to deny the suave working of divine providence." Nevertheless, since he thought that Saint Thomas was satisfied with a general call, he concluded that a general call "may also satisfy us." Augustine, however, also felt that "an ambiguous use of terms seems . . . to have caused some divergency of opinion," for while "the invitation to the higher life is extended to all . . . the actual choice of the religious state seems to

---

(100) "Codex questionem solvere noluisse videtur, et inter utramque opinionem medium iter tenuisse; canon enim 538 praeter externas qualitates negativas et positivas, internum etiam quoddam elementum requirit ut quis in religionem admitti possit, *rectam* nempe *intentionem*. Nobis auctorum dissensus magis verbalis esse videtur quam realis, et ex aequivoca terminologia *vocationis specialis* et *generalis* oriri (italics are the author's).

Certe nunc, quaevis opinio admittatur, in religionem licite et valide recipi potest quicumque liber ab impedimentis cuiusvis generis recta intentione ductus ut admittatur postulat; itemque licite ut admittatur postulat liber ab impedimentis recta ductus intentione; *indifferens vero est utrum hic dicatur specialem habere vocationem an solum generalem*" (italics inserted). —*Institutiones*, I, 703-704. The author, however, qualifies this observation in a note and shows that he leans towards the general vocation theory, for he refers to the Code as seeming to substantiate this preference: "Sunt tamen in Codice quaedam elementa quae se ad hanc questionem referunt. Ita c. 1353 supponit requiri et dari vocationem ad statum clericalem; quod non supponit, pro statu religioso c. 538.—*op. cit.*, p. 703, note (6).

(101) *Institutiones Iuris Canonici* (2 vols., Vol. I, 2. ed., Santander: Sal Terrae, 1946), I, n. 686, p. 363 (hereafter cited *Institutiones*).

(102) *Manuale*, p. 268, q. 200.

proceed from either efficacious or sufficient grace, no matter how we look at the working of that mysterious divine impulse." (103)

Cappello agrees with Augustine and Coronata regarding the ambiguous use of terms in this matter, and says that they are in error who think that canon 538 excludes the notion of a special vocation simply because it makes no explicit mention of such, for the right intention which the law does require is either the equivalent of a special vocation or necessarily a presupposition of it, and therefore "it must be said that also for the religious state (in addition to the priesthood) there is required a *special* vocation, which consists in the special movement of divine grace manifested at least through a right intention." (104)

Berutti, who emphasizes the difference between the private and public states of perfection, may be cited as holding the same opinion as regards the *juridic religious state*, and also agrees that to prove the existence of this special divine vocation in candidates "it is required and suffices that legitimate superiors prudently judge that the conditions or qualities exhaustingly enumerated in canon 538 are truly present in these candidates." (105) Vidal (1867-1938) also was very explicit in demanding the presence of a special divine call to the religious state, but by it he meant more than the movement of divine grace effecting the right intention, for he contended that, even though an aspirant has a right intention (a juridic requirement) along with the other elements of canon 538, one may not without temerity (although still apart from *grave* sin) enter the religious state as it exists today, unless one has received a *special* internal grace, actually given to relatively few persons, by which the Divine Will is made known to one. From the general invitation of Our Lord to pursue perfection, one cannot argue to a general invitation to enter the religious state, because the religious state today does not consist merely in following the counsels, but also includes the assuming of additional and perpetual obligations by irrevocable vow, which assumption of duties postulates the need for a special internal grace, and ecclesiastical superiors must have proof of at least its probable existence in a candidate before they may admit him to profession. (106)

While it would be of interest to examine the views of other canonists on the divine call to the religious life, essentially they add little to the various opinions already set down in these pages. (107) The authors cited give sufficient indica-

(103) *A Commentary on the New Code of Canon Law* (8 vols., Vol. III, 2. ed., St. Louis: Herder, 1919), pp. 199-200 (hereafter cited *Commentary*).

(104) *Tractatus Canonico-Moralis De Sacramentis* (5 vols., Vol. IV, 2. ed., Romae: Marietti, 1947), IV, n. 369, p. 263 (hereafter cited *De Sacramentis*). Italics are the author's.

(105) *Institutiones Iuris Canonici* (6 vols., Vol. III, Taurini-Romae: Marietti, 1936), III, 130 (hereafter cited *Institutiones*).

(106) *De Religiosis*, n. 239, pp. 188-190.

(107) Creusen, for example, points out the fact that grace alone can inspire the thoughtful and constant will to serve God more perfectly through the practice of the evangelical counsels, and this will is therefore a sign of the divine invitation. But he does not go into the

tion in their interpretations of canon 538 of the lack of unanimity which exists among them in this matter, and their various opinions serve as a convenient introduction and foundation for the writer's own conclusion of the *legislator's* stand on the question of divine religious vocation, which view is now presented simply as a legal guide or norm, not as an answer to the speculative problem.

At the outset it is readily admitted that since a divine vocation is *essentially* something intangible, a grace, (108) its existence is subject neither to immediate scrutiny nor to direct proof. Indeed, this point needs special emphasis, for a failure to grasp it would in all probability lead one into unwarranted exaggerations akin to those of the untenable attraction theory. Nevertheless, a divine vocation is not only a fact with theological implications, but as has been pointed out, it is also a fact of definite concern to the legislator *as a legislator*, who in regulating admission into the religious state must at the same time give to individuals the freedom which is rightfully theirs and yet must likewise obey in full the Divine Will in the matter. That the legislator has shown himself cognizant of the necessity for a divine vocation, and that he has demanded its presence in aspirants to the religious state, canon 538 clearly evinces when it lists a right intention among the qualifications which must be possessed by such persons, for it has been sufficiently demonstrated that a "*propositum religionis*" is impossible except through the direct action of God in the realm of grace. Simply, to require a right intention is to require a divine vocation, as Cappello has stated and Augustine has implied. Prümmer's observation, therefore, that the Code of Canon Law, while it speaks of a right intention, maintains a deep silence about a divine vocation cannot be upheld, and likewise the statement of Coronata that canon 538 does not suppose a divine vocation to be required is definitely erroneous as it stands, although from the context of the passage immediately preceding this statement, which is contained in a note, by vocation here he probably is referring to a special call. (109)

Moreover, the right intention, or divine vocation, is definitely a juridic consideration as well as a theological one. Since the requirement is explicitly mentioned in the law, this statement would seem superfluous were it not true in the words of Blat that, "since this intention is something internal, authors have been found who say that this is a requirement pertaining to conscience and moral

---

question of whether this will is the effect of a divine predilection or the efficacious result of man's free will cooperating with a grace which is given to all men. He does say, however, that "the presence of an obtacle which the subject cannot do away with of his own accord, or the lack of aptitude, would suffice to show that this desire is the result of a call to a more perfect life in general, and not of a vocation to the religious life in particular."—Creusen-Garesché-Ellis, *Religious Men and Women in the Code*, n. 170, p. 129.

(108) Cf. *supra*, pp. 34-36. Particular attention should be given to note (10) on page 35.

(109) Cf. *Institutiones*, I, n. 564, p. 703.

theology, and not juridic, since it escapes the vigilance of superiors." (110) He then goes on to say that "nevertheless we think it is also juridic, because from previous information, from the way the candidate bears himself, from his dealings with others, etc., a sound or a false intention can be detected, and having relied on this canon, superiors are able to refuse him admittance." (111) Beste, therefore, in calling the right intention a "theological requisite" without considering its juridic aspect is not completely accurate. Neither, it has been seen, are Schaefer, Cocchi and Ramstein, and particularly are the latter two authors erroneous when they leave to the conscience of the individual alone the judgment regarding the intention.

As expressed in canon 538, therefore, the discipline governing admission into the religious state definitely requires positive evidence of the presence of a divine vocation in a candidate, manifested at least through his right intention, before it permits his acceptance into that state. But what of the special-general vocation problem? Is the presence of this divine vocation the effect of God's special predilection, choosing some men in preference to others, or is it the efficacious result of man's cooperation with a grace which is made available to all? What is the legislator's position on this vital point?

The writer holds that the legislator *as legislator* has kept himself completely neutral on the controversy, that he has given a practical norm of action which demands positive evidence of the presence of a divine vocation (a right intention), but leaves the speculative problem of its specific nature in the speculative domain, to be examined and answered by the theologians. (112) In substantiation of this view, it is pointed out that the schema of canon 538, in contrast to its definitive form, was constructed in this wise:

> In religionem admitti potest quilibet catholicus qui nullo legitimo detineatur impedimento ac divina vocatione rectaque intentione moveatur. (113)

Now, had this law in its final revision retained the term "divine vocation" along with its requirement of right intention, Vidal, among others, in demanding a *special* internal grace in addition to the four qualifications enumerated by canon 538, (114) would have here a very strong argument in his favor. But while the authors who hold for the necessity of a special vocation may still present a cogent proof to verify their thesis, the point here stressed is that their thesis must be substantiated by evidence other

---

(110) *Commentarium Textus Codicis Iuris Canonici* (5 vols. in 6, Vol. II, Pars II et III, 3. ed., Romae: Collegio Angelico, 1938), II, Pars II et III, 270 (hereafter cited *Commentarium*).

(111) *Loc. cit.*

(112) This opinion is in accord with that which Coronata expresses in the body of his text on the question, and this has already been seen (*supra*, pp. 55-56), but it has also been noted that the author qualifies his statement somewhat by expressing his preference for the general vocation theory, and points to the comparative phrasing of canons 538 and 1353 to substantiate his choice (*supra*, p. 56, note 100).

(113) *Schema Codicis Iuris Canonici*, canon 412.

than that which is furnished by the law regarding the admission of candidates to the religious state as that law stands today in the Code. For the legislator has chosen to delete the key phrase which would argue so well for the truth of their opinion, and instead has kept only the term which demands the presence of a divine vocation, but which at the same time can be interpreted to fit in nicely with either the special or the general divine vocation theory. To the writer this considered action of the legislator is a convincing indication of the stand he wishes to take on the matter of divine religious vocation: he gives due recognition to that which is theologically certain, the necessity for a divine call, but so expresses that reality as to remain entirely neutral on the problem of its specific nature, a matter as yet theologically uncertain, his statement being acceptable to both sides of the controversy. It is a position which, for a legislator, is at once both practical and logical.

Carr, therefore, in saying, "that the words '*divina vocatione*' were subsequently deleted in the restatement of this canon seems to indicate an intention on the part of the legislator to reserve the concept of divine vocation specifically and exclusively for the priesthood," (115) is, in the opinion of the writer, going too far in his interpretation of the action. Such a statement really is no more than a gratuitous assumption, which may be gratuitously denied, and the same may be said of the interpretation of other authors, e.g., of Beste, of Regatillo, and of Prümmer, when they equate the four elements expressed in canon 538 exclusively with the notion of a general vocation. The truth of the matter is that the law itself does not make this equation, but fits in just as well with the special vocation theory. Both theories must include the elements of canon 538; the canon in its expression does not exclude the possibility of either theory's correctness; it simply does not choose between them. Cappello, therefore, is perfectly sound in his criticism of those authors who think that the legislator has excluded the notion of a special vocation in canon 538 for the reason simply that he has not explicitly mentioned it. On the other hand, Cappello goes to the opposite extreme by reading too much into the term "right intention" when he states that it is either the equivalent of or the necessary presupposition for a *special* divine call. (116) Once again, perhaps the right intention *is* the efficacious result of God's special predilection: but then perhaps it is not. The legislator does not say; he asks only that the right intention be present, no matter how it is formed.

Such an observation as that made by Bouscaren-Ellis, therefore, that in canon 538 "the legislator sums up the essential conditions and the sufficient signs of vocation to the religious life," (117) is a perfectly true statement, with which

(114) *Loc. cit.*

(115) *Vocation to the Priesthood*, p. 56. It has already been pointed out that Carr illogically espouses the general vocation concept. Cf. *supra*, p. 41, note (35).

(116) Cf. *supra*, p. 57. Berutti (*supra*, p. 57) is subject to the same criticism.

(117) *Loc. cit.*

proponents of either the special or the general divine vocation theory should have no quarrel. In like manner, any conclusion about the reality of and necessity for a divine vocation in candidates which holds that "it is required and suffices that legitimate superiors prudently judge that the conditions or qualities exhaustively enumerated in canon 538 are truly present in these candidates," (118) should raise no objection either. What is objected to, however, is reading more into the legislator's mind than that which he has actually expressed in the phrasing of his law on admission into the religious state. Canon 538 presents a practical norm of judgment and action in the face of a theological controversy; more than that the legislator has neither intended nor given.

The importance of this position and its practical application shall be treated in the final chapter of this study. Before concluding the present section, however, the writer wishes to make three important observations. The first is directed to those who profess the general vocation theory, and is simply a word of caution lest conviction of the truth of their thesis should lead them to a position which, by discrediting entirely or deriding the possibility of the manifestation of God's Will in a special (sometimes very special) manner, would amount to placing a limit on divine action. Such a position is, of course, untenable, historically as well as theologically, for not only can God distribute His gifts of grace to whomsoever He will, apart from any consideration of the merits of the individual, attracting some more strongly and making them more likely candidates for the religious state than others, but, as is commonly known, history is not without many such examples of special acts of Divine Providence. That the legislator is perfectly aware of the fact that even most extraordinary graces can be given has already been noted in the reply of the Commission of Cardinals who examined Canon Lahitton's work, which reply stated that a positive impulse of the Holy Spirit, or internal attraction of the subject, is not ordinarily given. (119)

It is also to be remembered, in the words of Pope Pius XII, that:

> . . . a vocation call of life is felt in the most diverse ways, corresponding to the infinitely diverse modulations of the voice of God; it may be an overpowering call, affectionately inviting inspiration, or gentle impulse—but the young Catholic girl, too, *who remains unmarried perforce*, trusting nonetheless the providence of Our Heavenly Father, *recognizes in the vicissitudes of life the call of the Master:* The Master is come and calleth for thee (John, 11-28). She hearkens. She gives up the fond dream of her adolescence and youth to have a faithful companion in life and set up a family. And in the exclusion of Matrimony she recognizes her vocation. Then, with a sorrowful but submissive heart, she too gives herself up to the noble and most diversified good works. (120)

---

(118) Berutti, *loc. cit.* It has already been observed, however, that in its context this statement refers to a special vocation, which the author requires for the juridic religious state.

(119) Cf. *supra*, p. 43, the implication, of course, being that it is given sometimes, at least.

(120) Allocutio, *Questa grande vostra*, 21 oct. 1945—*AAS*, XXXVII (1945), 287 (NCWC translation, p. 5). Italics inserted.

In other words, the call of God to any state in life (121) can find expression in the particular circumstances in which a person may find himself, as well as in other external indications, prohibiting action in one direction and seemingly encouraging action in another. With reference to the religious state, in view of the qualifications the Church may require at the time of a candidate's petition for admission, and which through no fault of his own he may not possess, the particular application is evident. While he might indeed have a right intention, "the presence of an obstacle which the subject cannot do away with of his own accord, or the lack of aptitude, would suffice to show that this desire is the result of a call to a more perfect life in general, and not of a vocation to religious life in particular." (122) In short, the advocates of the general vocation theory must realize that, even if their contention is the correct one, the word "general" is to be taken in a relative sense, as qualified according to the foregoing considerations.

The second observation is also expressed in a word of caution and is directed to the proponents of the special vocation theory. They should recall that the untenable attraction theory grew out of a false exaggeration of the legitimate opinion which they hold, and they should beware lest, in the presentation of that opinion, they lead those who are unskilled in the fine points of theology to confuse the two. If their theory is identifiable with the actually true doctrine, the positive signs of a divine vocation are still those of which mention is made in canon 538. The legislator does not demand more, and neither should they. Indeed, the legislator's use of the term "*quilibet catholicus*" seems a strong indication of his mind as regards placing too severe a restriction on those who desire to follow the evangelical counsels in the juridic religious state, and in this regard, too, it might properly be pointed out that Saint Thomas, who held to the special vocation theory, saw so close a parallel between vocation to the religious state and to the Christian life in general, that he could argue that a man is no more to be dissuaded from following a religious vocation from fear of possible defection, than one is to be prevented from embracing the faith because of the chance of later apostasy. (123)

And finally the advocates of both theories must be careful not to make too sweeping generalizations or to draw faulty conclusions from the references to vocation which they may find in the decrees, constitutions, instructions, etc., emanating from the Holy See since the Code of Canon Law. As with the pre-Code legislation, they must realize that the legislator may give indications of his

(121) The passage quoted above has special reference to the state of the unmarried laywoman in the world. For a good analysis of this allocution of Pius XII cf. Faherty, *The Destiny of Modern Women in the Light of Papal Teaching* (Westminster, Md.: Newman, 1950), pp. 109-167, *passim*.

(122) Creusen-Garesché-Ellis, *loc. cit.* Cf. also *supra*, p. 35, note (10).

(123) Cf. Farrell, *Theology of Religious Vocation*, p. 43, note (4).

theological convictions upon uncertain matters, without forcing them upon those who do not subscribe to them. And particularly must the proponents of the special vocation theory beware, lest they argue from the legislator's recognition of a special call from God in some instances, to the fact that he insists upon such in all cases. (124)

This much, then, is certain: Christ has a definite plan for His Mystical Body, and in that plan religious have a definite role, the efficacious fulfillment of which will come about through man's cooperation with divine grace. Just how the doctrine of efficacious grace is to be reconciled with human liberty remains a theological controversy, but a controversy which presents no practical difficulty in the question of religious vocation, for the legislator, while requiring a divine call, has offered a practical norm of judgment in canon 538, by which its presence may be detected, a norm which may confidently be followed by superiors and candidates alike, no matter to which vocation theory they may subscribe. God's providence is not wanting.

(124) The present Holy Father, for example, has on a number of occasions indicated the special workings of Divine Providence in the matter of an individual's choice of a state of life. Cf., for instance, these statements: "But the good Lord . . . so disposed that . . . there have been and are now great numbers of chosen souls who not only burn with the desire of individual perfection, but who, while by a special vocation from God they remain in the world, are able to find excellent new forms of Consociation . . . in which they can lead a life very well adapted to the acquirement of Christian perfection."—Pius XII, const. *Provida Mater Ecclesiae*, 2 febr. 1947 (*AAS*, XXXIX [1947], 117) (translation by Bouscaren, *The Canon Law Digest* [2 vols. and Supplement through 1948, Milwaukee: The Bruce Publishing Company, 1934-1949], Supplement, p. 67); ". . . even in the world, with a special vocation from God and with the help of divine grace, it is certainly possible to attain a rather strict and effective self-consecration to God."—*ibidem*, p. 118 (Bouscaren, *op. cit.*, p. 68); "The Holy Spirit . . . has called to Himself by a great and special grace many beloved sons and daughters . . . to the end that, being united and organized in Secular Institutes, they may be the salt of the earth."—motu propr. *De Institutione Saecularium Laude atque Confirmatione*, 12 mart. 1948 (*AAS*, XL [1948]), 283-284 (*Bouscaren, op. cit.*, p. 76); "To the moderators and assistants of Catholic action and of other Associations of the faithful, in whose maternal bosom are being trained to full Christian living and introduced to the exercise of the apostolate so many chosen young people who are called by divine vocation to a higher life either in Religious Institutes and Societies of common life or in Secular Institutes, we recommend with fatherly affection that they generously promote such holy Vocations."—*ibidem*, p. 286 (Bouscaren, *op. cit.*, pp. 79-80). But cf. also his words to the representatives of Italian youth after he had spoken at length on the great need today of vocation to the life of consecrated service, "Qui potest capere capiat: let him accept it who can: we wish to cry out to Catholic boys and girls, taking Christ's words in the sense of an invitation and encouragement (Qui potest capere capiat: Chi può capire, capisca: vorremmo gridare ai giovani e alle giovani cattoliche, prendendo le parole di Christo in senso di invito e di incoraggiamento)."—Allocutio ad puellas ab actione catholica ex Italiae diocesibus Romae coadunatas, 24 apr. 1943 (*AAS*, XXXV [1943], 136).

CHAPTER V

THE ECCLESIASTICAL VOCATION TO THE JURIDIC RELIGIOUS STATE

The substance of what has been seen in the preceding pages concerning the divine call to the juridic religious state is, of course, equally applicable to the religious life in its primordial sense, the life of perfection as established by Christ, with the added essential and accidental elements of the presently existing public state prescinded from. (1) Each state has self-perfection as its primary end and the evangelical counsels as its primary means; each must be embraced with a right intention and necessarily, therefore, under the impetus of divine grace. Consequently, the question of divine vocation in both instances raises the same problem about the specific nature of that call, whether it is special or general, and in both finds the same practical solution: *all other things being equal*, the actual presence of a right intention in a subject, no matter how one chooses to reconcile the doctrine of efficacious grace with man's free will, is sufficient evidence in a particular instance of God's invitation to one or the other state, and man may confidently and meritoriously act upon it. (2)

With reference to the private and individual pursuit of perfection, the phrase "all other things being equal" does not demand extensive comment. It is true, of course, that an individual may himself have placed an obstacle in the way of carrying out his present desire of embracing the religious life in its *complete* primordial sense. One who has contracted marriage, for example, is bound in justice to fulfill the obligations of the state he has entered, obligations which are incompatible with a vow of perfect chastity, (3) and therefore while he can

(1) Cf. *supra*, pp. 11-18.

(2) The same thing, of course, is true *a pari* of the other canonical states of perfection, the so-called "quasi-religious" societies and secular institutes. Cf. *supra*, p. 32, note (85).

(3) Adopting the common usage to be found especially among moral and ascetical writers of recent times, the present writer to avoid confusion has used (and shall continue to use) the terms *chastity* and *perfect chastity* as being synonymous with continence or the complete abstention from the exercise of sex, legitimate as well as illegitimate. He wishes to state, however, that he deems the usage an unhappy one, not only because it is inexact, but also because it may very well tend to debase the dignity of Christian marriage, and bring that divine institution into discredit, as if it were true that married people cannot be chaste, or at least are only imperfectly so. This is in fact implied by the writer of the article on chastity in the *Dictionnaire de Théologie Catholique* (Vol. II, col. 2,319). He defines chastity as the virtue which inclines one to abstain from all carnal delectation, *even that permitted in the state of marriage* (*!*).

The truth of the matter, of course, is that the virtue of chastity *does not exclude* the exercise of the sex function, but rather *moderates its use* in accordance with right reason. Now, right reason indicates complete abstention from the exercise of sex in the unmarried, but it does

still strive for and attain the highest perfection, the means at his disposal do not include *all* the essential elements of the primordial religious state in its strict sense, (4) and consequently he is prohibited from becoming a religious even in that sense. Or to put the matter more precisely, he has already made a free choice concerning his state in life, a choice which demands that he pursue perfection in one direction and not in another. (5)

Moreover, it must not be overlooked particularly with regard to the vow of chastity, that not all lawful things are expedient. (6) While it is true in the words of Pope Leo XIII that "in choosing a state of life, it is indisputable that all are at full liberty either to follow the counsel of Jesus Christ as to virginity, or to

---

not imply such abstention in those who are married, and chastity, therefore, is quite compatible with the use of sex within the married state. Simply, there are two kinds of chastity: conjugal chastity, proper to persons living in lawful wedlock, and continence, proper to the unmarried. In view of the wrong inference which, concerning the chastity of the married state, can be drawn from the common use of the term, it seems preferable to define chastity as the virtue which moderates the exercise of sex in accordance with right reason, and then to characterize this virtue according to the various states of life, in which right reason diversifies its dictates. The evangelical counsel of perfection would then be seen in its true light, as not chastity precisely, but complete abstention from the exercise of sex, i.e., perfect continence, and the honor and dignity of both marriage and virginity would be enhanced thereby.

St. Thomas was indeed very much to the point when he stated that, "although virginity is better than conjugal continence, it may happen nevertheless that a married person is better than a virgin," and he thereupon quoted St. Augustine, who instructed a virgin to say: "I am not better than Abraham, but celibate chastity is better than the chastity of marriage." —*Summa Theologica*, IIa, IIae, q. 152, a. 4, ad. 2. And in the next article of the same question St. Thomas insisted that, while virginity is the most excellent in its own category, i.e., as a form of chastity, inasmuch as it transcends the chastity of widowhood and marriage, virginity itself is not the most excellent virtue of all.—*Ibidem*, a. 5. Cf. also Messenger, *Two in One Flesh*, Vol. I, pp. 7-9, Vol. II, pp. 10-11; Tanquerey-Branderis, *The Spiritual Life, A Treatise on Ascetical and Mystical Theology* (2. ed., Tournai: Desclée and Co., 1930), pp. 518-521 (hereafter cited *The Spiritual Life*).

(4) Cf. *supra*, pp. 13-14.

(5) His life may, of course, surpass in perfection even that of the greatest "religious" saint. Such an achievement is not impossible. But the centuries-old experience of the Church has proven that the *surest* and *quickest* way to perfection is to lay an axe to the obstacles and distractions in the way of a completely free embrace of God, and this the *three* vows of poverty, chastity and obedience do in a most marvelous manner (cf. *supra*, pp. 13-14). The religious is like a skilled alpinist, who in his eagerness to reach the heights casts off all unnecessary burdens, but this act of renunciation does not imply that wealth, marriage, or freedom are evil in any way; rather it is a declaration that in comparison with the love of God nothing is much good. Cf. the whole of chapter seven of St. Paul's *First Epistle to the Corinthians* for a clear concise treatment and comparison of the states of marriage and virginity. The Apostle does not say that celibacy is necessarily holiness, or married life necessarily worldliness, but he points out the opportunities of the one, and the dangers of the other.

(6) Cf. I Cor., VI, 12.

enter the bonds of marriage," (7) and that God will not allow a person to be tempted beyond his strength to resist, (8) still it is common knowledge that a life of perpetual continence presents a much graver problem for some men than for others. The frequency as well as the violence of temptations against chastity varies greatly among individuals, and this for a variety of reasons, differences in temperament, in character, in education and in one's background of discipline being but a few of the causes. Therefore, even though one who finds continence a very severe trial cannot be forced into marriage, (9) it seems the better part of prudence, at least for most men of such passionate nature, not to have one's eternal salvation depend upon the exercise of heroic virtue, when the legitimate remedies of the secondary ends of marriage might offer an easier solution to the particular problem. Such a one, therefore, at least should not act hastily in binding himself to the perpetual observance of continence, nor assume the obligation without seeking advice and direction on the matter. (10)

Nevertheless, giving these important considerations their due recognition, one is still correct in saying that a man of good will may embrace the private state of evangelical perfection on his own volition, i.e., in assuming the divine invitation of grace, he needs no further invitation from anyone. In other words, as regards the personal and individual pursuit of perfection, the observation which Saint Hippolytus made at the beginning of the third century still has pertinent application today: "Personal choice [or one's own free will] alone is that which makes a virgin." (11) For while Our Lord has indeed entrusted to

(7) Ep. encycl. *Rerum novarum*, 15 maii 1891—*ASS*, XXIII (1890-91), 645, translation contained in *Five Great Encyclicals* (New York: Paulist Press, 1939), p. 5. Pope Pius XI (1922-1939) quoted his statement in his encyclical *Casti connubii*, 31 dec. 1930—*AAS*. XXII (1930), 542.

(8) Cf. I Cor., X, 13.

(9) Regarding the frequency and violence of temptation, "God's providential designs must also be taken into account. There are souls whom He destines for a holy calling and whose purity He shelters with a jealous care. *There are others whom He likewise destines to sanctity, but whom He would have pass through severe tests in order to ground them in virtue.* Lastly others there are whom He does not destine to such a high vocation, and who will be more or less frequently tempted, but never beyond their strength."—Tanquerey-Branderis, *The Spiritual Life*, p. 429 (italics inserted).

(10) Cf. what St. Paul in the seventh chapter of his *First Epistle to the Corinthians* has to say on this point: " . . . it is good for man not to touch woman. Yet for fear of fornication, let each man have his own wife, and let each woman have her own husband."—vv. 1-3; "But I say to the unmarried and to widows, it is good for them if they remain, even as I. But if they do not have self-control, let them marry, for it is better to marry than to burn (with passion)."—vv. 8-10. The question of the difficulty of continence has a very particular application to the juridic religious state, and shall be seen in its proper place.

(11) Dix, *Apostolic Tradition*, p. 21. Even more explicit is the "Testament of Our Lord," a seventh century Syriac translation of a lost fourth or fifth century Greek expansion and adaptation of Hippolytus' treatise: "A male or female virgin is not instituted or appointed by man, but is voluntarily separated and named. But a hand is not laid upon him as for virginity. But this separation is of (his) own free will."—*loc. cit.*

His Church the direction of the faithful in the way of the counsels as well as in the path of the precepts, (12) and canonical legislation has declared the effects of certain private vows, (13) the Church nowhere requires its own or anyone else's permission before one can validly and licitly embrace the evangelical counsels in a private way. (14)

The same thing, however, is not by any means true with regard to the public state of perfection, and here precisely is had the point of departure at which the concept of vocation to the juridic religious state takes leave of its counterpart to the primordial religious state. One may here anticipate, for the sake of contrast, what shall be demonstrated: although the Church has never prohibited any of its children from striving after the perfection counseled by Christ, at the same time adopting and giving legal recognition to the earliest monastic practice, the Church has ever insisted on a process of discrimination to be employed in the selection of candidates for the public religious state, allowing only those to be admitted who after strict examination and probation measure up to the *norms established by law*. In other words, vocation to the life of evangelical perfection in itself and vocation to the juridic religious state are not (and never have been) mutually coextensive: Christ's invitation is seen as an essential part, but not as the sum and substance, of a vocation to the juridic religious life for it is a fact that no one can be a religious in the juridic sense unless he first is accepted and invited to profession in a lawfully constituted institute by a legitimate superior, who judges a candidate's suitability according to legally established norms. It is this latter invitation, without which a religious vocation does not exist, which constitutes the ecclesiastical call to the religious state, and if truth is to be preserved and the *complete* concept of religious vocation is to be had, it is of the greatest importance that this call be understood for what it is and seen in its proper perspective, without overemphasis but also without underestimate.

---

(12) Cf. *supra*, p. 16, note (22).

(13) Marriage, for example, is rendered illicit in the face of the simple vows of virginity of perfect chastity, of not marrying, of the receiving of sacred orders, and of the embracing of the religious state. Cf. canon 1058.

(14) Whether or not the Church *could* do so is a moot point, involving among other things the question of the Church's jurisdiction over internal acts. On this cf. Ottaviani, *Institutiones Iuris Publici Ecclesiastici* (2 vols., Vol. I, 3. ed., Romae: Typis Polyglottis Vaticanis, 1947), I, 243-249; Tanquerey, *Synopsis Theologiae Moralis et Pastoralis* (3 vols., Vol. II, 10. ed., Parisiis, Tornaci, Romae: Desclée et Socii, 1936), II, 196-198. The Church, of course, can dispense from vows (cans. 1309, 1313); vows can also be annulled by one who exercises dominative power over the will of the person making the vow, suspended by one who has power over the matter of the vow (can. 1312), as well as commuted by those to whom the law gives that power (cf. can. 1314). Cf. Bouscaren-Ellis, *Commentary*, pp. 674-676; Coronata, *Institutiones*, II, 223-231.

Article I. The Nature and Intrinsic Necessity of the Ecclesiastical Vocation to the Juridic Religious State

Considerable space has been devoted in the third chapter of this study to the development of the religious life from its primordial nature to the public religio-social state as it exists at present. There it was emphasized that, while the primary end and means of the religious life have never changed, the canonical state of perfection, by ecclesiastical creation one of the three principal states in the Church today, encompasses within its ambit not only the means to personal sanctification, (15) but elements which directly contribute to the glory and welfare of both society and the Church as a whole. Religious not only follow the evangelical counsels for themselves, but living and working together as a special ecclesiastical order of canonical persons, juridically recognized and privileged, they stand before men as the Church's official representatives in the life of perfection, persons who have obtained special and public deputation to divine worship. In addition, and this also in law as well as in fact, religious are utilized by the Church to serve as conduits of divine truth and mercy, aiding the Church in this way to fulfill its mission in the fields of education, social service, conversion of heretics, missionary activity, etc., and as it happens, for so many they represent *the* educational and charitable activity of the Church.

Now it is precisely this aspect of the religious life, its nature as an *official corporate organization of the life of perfection and public service in the Church*, that gives rise to and, indeed, necessitates the ecclesiastical call to the religious state, in addition to the divine call. In the first place, the Church presents the juridic religious state with its means of acquiring perfection in common as the best possible response to Christ's desire for all men to be perfect. It enters into a bilateral contract with the religious which, in exchange for the right to utilize his faculties of soul and body, binds the Church to direct the religious in the way of perfection by providing for his spiritual needs as well as temporal necessities. (16) As a consequence of this obligation which it has assumed, the Church, acting through duly constituted representatives, must see to the prevention and elimination of all elements which might impede the spiritual progress of those who have submitted themselves to its care, and certainly foremost among its concerns in this regard must be its careful selection of only fit and suitable persons among the aspirants to the religious state.

Eliminating at the outset those who petition entrance with an evil intention and whose immoral and irresponsible lives manifest the lack of a divine vocation, an admitting superior must also take into consideration the peculiar nature of the common life and weigh the qualifications of candidates accordingly. Life

(15) It should not be forgotten, however, that an individual's spiritual well-being contributes to the supernatural welfare of every member of the mystical body. Cf. *supra*, pp. 17-18.

(16) Cf. *supra*, pp. 31-32.

in community, besides requiring an obedient submission to lawful authority, demands a certain "give and take" among fellow members, often a refining of likes and dislikes, and certainly a special regard and consideration for others. It is not the life for an individualist who is either unable or unwilling to cooperate with the requirements it imposes, and who in the expression of his individualism can easily disturb the internal peace and good order necessary for the spiritual advancement of the group. While such a one might be very well suited for an eremitical form of life, it is neither for the benefit of himself nor for the good of the community that he be allowed membership in the juridic religious state as it exists today, embracing as that state does a life that is led in common. In short, considering the nature of the common life and the Church's obligations towards those noble souls who have embraced it, the Church must practice a process of discrimination in admitting candidates into the religious state.

But an even more important cause for such discrimination among religious aspirants is the Church's concern, not only for the well-being of a particular community, but for the welfare of the entire religious state with its concomitant effect for good or evil on the Church and society themselves. A religious by the very fact that he is a recognized member of the canonical state of perfection, represents for those with whom he comes into contact "the life of religion" and, particularly by non-Catholics, he is seen as a special envoy of the Church itself. Indeed, his very dress singles him out as someone special in the Church, and there are few who would express surprise to learn that the Church officially regards his state in life as one to be esteemed and honored, (17) or that he is the recipient of many privileges not enjoyed by the laity. As a consequence of the unique position which he thus has, both in law and in fact, as has already been pointed out, the good which a religious accomplishes is attributed to the entire religious state and to the Church, and redounds to their glory and benefit; conversely, and no matter how unjust the attribution, the evil or harm which he may cause will reflect back to them also. It is easily recognized, therefore, why care must be exercised that only those candidates be admitted into the religious state who are acceptable representatives both of the Church and of the particular religious institute they desire to enter. The common good demands it.

It is true that some of the prescriptions which have to be enacted from time to time to preserve this common good will appear to many to be irksome and inconvenient, not to say even severe on occasion. A reformed public sinner, for example, can become the greatest of saints, and he certainly is not to be denied the pursuit of evangelical perfection. But while his conversion of morals and good intentions are indeed commendable, depending on circumstances, e.g., the era or the locality, they might not remove the danger of the giving of scandal to the world at large, which often does not understand such things, and his acceptance into a religious institute could bring down opprobrium upon the

(17) Cf. can. 487.

religious state itself and hamper its power for good in the world. In such a case, the common good of the religious state and the Church must take precedence over the private good that such an individual can obtain by being received into the canonical state of perfection.

Another obvious example among many which can be given is that of illegitimacy. An illegitimate child certainly is not to blame for his unhappy status, and he may very well possess the highest type of moral and spiritual character. And yet here too the welfare of the whole religious state, which to a great extent depends upon the good estimation of society, must be considered. Especially in certain localities and in particular periods of history, the presence of illegitimates in a religious institute might be regarded with such suspicion or even disfavor by the populace as to bring discredit, however unjustly, to the religious state itself, and consequently the common good might have to decree that such a one be refused admission into it.

Moreover, as has been noted, the religious life exhibits a rich variety of spiritual trends and modes, each institute having its own particular approach to the common goal of perfection and being singularly distinguished in the pursuit of its secondary ends. As is to be expected, therefore, qualifications for admission can naturally differ from institute to institute. Consequently, an admitting superior must not only judge the sincerity of a candidate's intention to follow the evangelical counsels, but in addition must ask himself whether or not, in the light of the positive constitution and nature of his particular institute, it is to the general interest of that order, of the religious state, and of the Church itself that this applicant be admitted. Conditions of health, of character, and even of education may be required by a particular form of the religious life, although they are not thus demanded by the evangelical counsels taken in themselves, nor even by another institute, and even though the candidate has done well in offering himself, the answer of the superior to his request for admission could be in the negative, and justly so.

The matter may be reduced to this: if the Church is to act in accord with its obligations towards itself, towards society, and towards its children, the religious state, crystallized as it is into several orders and congregations of ecclesiastical origin, must be made a closed corporation, a reserved state. And since the Church is the source of the existence and the rights of these communities, it belongs to its own duly constituted agents to determine who will be permitted to enter, to become a member of a particular religious institute. Admittedly a superior might err in his judgment about a candidate's fitness for the religious state, and even unwarrantedly reject him. Nevertheless the common good directs that the practice be preserved, despite whatever loss an occasional individual might have to bear for being denied the benefits to be derived from participation in the canonical state of perfection. And with such an institute in existence, the conclusion logically follows that, since the private pursuit of perfection is no longer recognized as a canonical religious state, a candidate who has not been accepted by the competent superior in *some* approved order or congregation becomes under such circumstances debarred from entry into the religious state. He has no *religious* vocation, because he has not the ecclesiastical vocation.

This institute, of course, is not theoretical merely, but is clearly contained and specified in the practice of the Church as manifested in ecclesiastical legislation, past and present.

ARTICLE II. THE HISTORICAL BACKGROUND OF ECCLESIASTICAL VOCATION TO THE RELIGIOUS STATE

The Church's recognition in history of the necessity of a legitimate superior's "call" to the religious state is seen both in its explicit and implicit approbation of constitutional provisions for admission into the various institutes, thereby identifying its vocational concept with that of the private lawmaker, and in its own explicit legislation regarding such admission, thus further defining that concept within limited bounds.

1. The concept of vocation as found in the monastic Rules

Three religious Rules (18) are of particular historical importance to this study, the Rule of Saint Pachomius, because it was the first of the monastic Rules and greatly influenced subsequent Rules, the Rule of Saint Basil, because of its great influence on Oriental monasticism, not only in his own day, but through the centuries and even today, and especially the Rule of Saint Benedict, which from the ninth century until the twelfth was almost the only one in use in the Western Church, and upon which almost all the legislation of the Western councils of that period with relation to the monastic life was based. The concept of divine vocation to be found in these Rules has already been noted; (19) it is their influence on the crystallization of the concept of ecclesiastical vocation that is of interest here.

a. The Rule of Pachomius

The 49th chapter of the Rule of Pachomius reads as follows:

---

(18) The "Rule" in ecclesiastical law refers to the group of principles regarding the religious life proposed to their disciples by the first organizers of this kind of life. It is in this sense that one speaks of the Rule of Saint Basil, the Rule of Saint Benedict, etc. Each of the monastic institutes had a Rule, either one that was formulated by the founder himself, or, as was more often the case, one that was adapted, with more or less variation, from one of the older existing Rules. In contrast with the Rule thus understood, the "Constitutions" of an institute contain the laws which are characteristic of the different institutes which follow the same Rule. Since the sixteenth century a great many institutes have arisen which do not follow one of the ancient Rules, and in their case the Rules are called constitutions. Cf. Creusen-Garesché-Ellis, *Religious Men and Women*, n. 271, p. 204; Schaefer, *De Religiosis*, pp. 84, 95-97.

(19) Cf. *supra*, pp. 38-39; cf. also pp. 44-46.

Si quis accesserit ad ostium monasterii volens saeculo renuntiare, et fratrum aggregari numero, non habebit intrandi libertatem, sed prius nuntiabitur patri monasterii, et manebit paucis diebus foris ante ianuam, et docebitur orationem Dominicam ac psalmos, quantos poterit ediscere: et diligenter sui experimentum dabit, ne forte mali quidpiam fecerit et turbatus ad horam timore discesserit, aut sub aliqua potestate sit; et utrum possit renuntiare parentibus, et propriam contemnere facultatem. Si enim viderint aptum ad orationem et ad omnia tunc docebitur et reliquas monasterii disciplinas, quas servare debeat et facere, quibusque servire, sive in collecta omnium fratrum sive in domo cui tradendus est, sive in vescendi ordine; ut instructus atque perfectus in omni opere bono, fratribus copuletur. Tunc nudabunt cum vestimentis saecularibus et induent habitu monachorum, tradentque ostiario, ut orationis tempore adducat eum in conspectum omnium fratrum; sedebitque in loco in quo ei praeceptum fuerit. (20)

Here we have the explicit directions of the founder of monasticism for the reception, probation, and final admission of candidates into his community. The point to be emphasized is that one who had the will to renounce the world and to be numbered among the Pachomian monks, that is, one who wished to pursue the counsels of perfection in this particular community, while he might be free to seek after perfection on his own, he certainly was not free merely of his own volition to do so in the monasteries of Pachomius: "*non habebit intrandi libertatem.*"

In the first place, the candidate himself was not the one to pass definitive judgment on the rightness of his intention. That was subject to the rigid examination of others, and he would be refused admittance because of lack of proper intention if, for instance, he sought admission to escape persecution for crimes committed. Likewise he would not be accepted if he was a slave or for some other reason not his own master ("*sub aliqua potestate*"), or bound by parental ties which he was unable to renounce. Moreover, even if the candidate successfully passed his first scrutiny on these points, he still had to undergo a further period of probation during which he was taught the monastic discipline, what was to be expected of him, whom and how he was to obey, etc. He undoubtedly was watched very closely during this time for indications that would declare him unfit or unworthy to be numbered among the brethren as a monk, and it was only after he had been well instructed and "judged perfect in every good work" that he was allowed to take his place among them.

The length of time during which a candidate was to be tried and observed prior to his admission was not determined in the Pachomian Rule, but this is not an important consideration here. The very fact that he was tried at all and had to possess certain qualifications other than the will to follow the evangelical counsels is sufficient to show a definite singling out process in the acceptance of a candidate as a Pachomian monk. Just who it was in the Pachomian system who made the definitive judgment as to the acceptance or refusal of a candidate is not explicitly stated in the Rule. Probably it was the local superior himself

(20) *Reg. S. Pachomii—MPL*, XXIII, 70.

acting on the advice of the monks who had the charge of watching over and instructing the candidate, for the Rule very definitely put the superior in charge in all things, and he had to be informed of the presence of the petitioner even before he was admitted into the monastery for his period of probation. (21)

b. The Rule of Basil

The aspirant to the religious life as practiced in the monasteries of Saint Basil had first to undergo the examination and possess the qualifications laid down in the Rule of that Holy Founder before being admitted to profession. His legislation on this point closely followed that of Saint Pachomius: there was to be the same testing of the spirit, the same exclusion of those of questionable morals, and the same provision for a period of probation in which the superior either accepted or rejected the candidate. While the qualifications demanded in the candidate might not appear to be too numerous or rigorous, again the important point here is that there were any requirements at all beyond the will of the individual to embrace the life of perfection. Some were chosen as fit and suitable to be a monk; others were not. Or to put it in another way: some were invited to make their profession in the Basilian foundation; others were not given the call to do so, although it must again be recalled that rejection would not prevent them from the individual pursuit of perfection, even through the three vows.

As to the negative requirements in the candidate demanded by Saint Basil, slaves could not be admitted, except under exceptional circumstances, (22) and married persons were likewise to be refused admission unless with reference to this matter there existed the mutual consent of the spouses. (23) On the positive side the candidate had to give ample proof of the sincerity of his intentions, and of the stability and integrity of his character, and he further had to give evidence that he was prepared to practice the virtues demanded of a Basilian monk. To ascertain this, not only was his past life carefully inquired into, but even after admission into the monastery the candidate had to undergo a period of proba-

(21) While the Rule of Saint Pachomius shows that discrimination among candidates was practiced from the very inception of monasticism, this is not to imply that the practice was not known in the religious life before then, for it was the rule even in the semi-eremitical type of life founded by Saint Anthony. No one who looks into the *Historia Lausiaca* would be inclined to say that entrance into that life was an easy affair. Paul the Simple (234-347), for example, was at first refused by Saint Anthony, and it was only after a very hard and difficult period of probation that he heard the welcome words of acceptance: "*In nomine Jesu, ecce factus es monachus.*" The implication throughout is that had Paul not successfully proven himself in the eyes of Anthony, he would not have been able to number himself among the Antonian monks, even though his intentions were of the best, and although he will still free to follow the evangelical counsels on his own. Cf. Palladius, *Historia Lausiaca*, c. 28—*MPL*, LXXIII, 1127-1128.

(22) *Reg. fus. tract.* 11—*MPG*, XXXI, 947.

(23) *Reg. fus. tract.* 12—*MPG*, XXXI, 947.

tion and careful scrutiny, during which time his fitness for the life of a monk was decided upon:

> Periculosum est repellere eos qui nostra opera accedunt ad Dominum . . . nec tamen permittendum est ut illotis pedibus ad sancta documenta veniat. (24)

Only those who were judged to possess the required qualifications were admitted by profession into the monastic community, the definite decision being made by the superior of the community with the advice particularly of those in whose care the candidate was placed during his period of probation.

c. The Rule of Benedict

The norms laid down by Saint Benedict regarding the admission of adult laymen into his monasteries show a close similarity to the ones adopted in the earlier monastic Rules in both the Eastern and the Western Church, especially those of Saint Pachomius. (25) Clearly realizing how important it was for all who were engaged in the pursuance of perfection under monastic discipline that applicants for admission be carefully screened, he explicitly ordered in his Rule that not all who applied were to be easily accepted without discrimination. Only those who gave evidence that they were sincere in their good intentions were to be admitted:

> Noviter veniens quis ad conversionem, non ei facilius tribuatur ingressus; sed sicut ait Apostolus: 'Probate spiritus, si ex Deo sunt.' (26)

As a preliminary trial, four or five days of patient and persistent petitioning outside the very doors of the monastery, and this in the face of difficulties and harsh treatment (*injuria*) heaped upon him by the monks, was demanded of the applicant, and only if he passed this test and was judged sincere was he to be admitted for a further and main period of probation. This period was to last for an entire year. In a place set apart and under the special care and direction of an older monk, he was taught all that is rugged and hard on the way to perfection and he was carefully observed "*si revera Deum quaerit, si sollicitus est ad opus Dei, ad obedientiam, ad opprobria.*" If after successfully having passed his year of probation he persevered in his intention and promised to submit himself in all things to the Rule, only then was the candidate finally admitted into the congregation by a formal profession before all the community. (27) Definite acceptance awaited the discretion of the abbot, who, as in all weighty matters, having first heard the views of the community called together in chapter, weighed the matter within himself and did what he thought best, (28) undoubtedly paying particular heed to the opinion of the novice master.

---

(24) *Reg. fus. tract.* 10—*MPG,* XXXI, 943-947; cf. the entire tract.

(25) Cf. *Concordia Regularum Patrum—MPL,* CIII, 702-1380, where parallel references to the various sources of the Benedictine Rule are clearly pointed out.

(26) *Regula,* c. 58—*MPL,* LXVI, 803.

(27) *Loc. cit.*

(28) *Regula,* c. 3—*MPL,* LXVI, 287-288.

These provisions in the Rule of Saint Benedict for the admission of candidates into the monastic life, substantially the same as those in the Rules of Saints Pachomius and Basil, and indicative of those set down in all religious Rules and constitutions before the Code of Canon Law, (29) make one thing very clear: entrance into a religious community was made dependent on much more than the mere purpose of the individual. He could be numbered among the members of a religious organization only if, tried and proven according to definitely established norms, he was accepted by legitimate authority.

2. The concept of religious vocation and ecclesiastical legislation

a. Before the Council of Trent (1545-1563)

It does not seem too gratuitous an assumption to suppose that, even before specific legislation demanded the scrutiny and approval of monastic Rules by ecclesiastical power, the bishops of the Church, as chief pastors and guardians of faith and morals in their territories, felt it incumbent upon themselves at least to become acquainted with these Rules, lest perhaps they contain in them anything heretical or dangerous. The bishops certainly were aware, therefore, of the provisions for admission into the monastic communities, and with at least their implicit approbation of the monastic Rules, there existed also the implicit acceptance of the concept of vocation which these rules created. Acceptance of the one without the other was not possible.

The Rule of Saint Benedict, moreover, was very early given explicit approbation by many local councils, (30) and the II Lateran Council (1139), a general council of the Church, in addition to the Rule of Saint Benedict, recognized also the Rules of Saint Basil and Saint Augustine. (31) The approbation of the entire Rule by that very fact included the approval of the chapters regulating the acceptance of the candidates. Therefore it needs only to be recalled that admission into the monastic community by Rule was made dependent upon the

(29) Naturally, according to circumstances, different times and places and the diversity of pursuits engaged in, qualifications for admission would be expected to differ among the various institutes. In the Rule of Saint Francis, for example, an applicant had first to prove his knowledge of the Catholic Faith and of the Sacraments before being admitted even to his period of probation, and (an innovation) the provincial superior alone, exclusive of all others, had the right to admit him into the novitiate. Previously such a matter had been left to the discretion of the local superior. Cf. *Secunda Regula B. Patris Francisci pro Fratribus Minoribus*, c. 2—*Codex Regularum Monasticarum et Canonicarum* (Tom. III, ed. Lucas Holstenius, Romae, 1759), III, 31.

(30) Cf. Germanic Council under Boniface (742), c. 7—Mansi, XII, 367; Conc. Leptinnes (743), c. 1—Mansi, XII, 371; Council of Aix-la-Chapelle (Aachen) (802), additio—Mansi, XIII, 1104; Council of Mainz (813), c. 11—Mansi, XIV, 68; II Council of Rheims (813), c. 22—Mansi, XIV, 98. These councils really had far more than "local" significance. They were among the chief sources of the Carolingian reform legislation which amounted to a more or less formal adoption of Benedictine Monasticism as *the* religious state in the Frankish Empire.

(31) C. 26—Mansi, XXI, 532.

acceptance on the part of legitimate superiors after they were satisfied with the candidate's fitness and suitability, and that only ecclesiastically authorized communities had legal recognition, logically to conclude that, juridically regarded, a vocation to the monastic life was recognized to have at least a partial and necessary source in the acceptance by a legitimate superior into an ecclesiastically approved institute.

Explicit ecclesiastical legislation on the entrance of candidates into the monastic life centered chiefly on the negative requirements or on the absence of impediments in the aspirant, and the period of probation (or novitiate) which he had to undergo before incorporation by profession into the community. The quantity of the legislation is not so much of concern here, as is the fact that any legislation existed at all which demanded more of the candidate than the mere purpose to accept the invitation of Christ to follow the evangelical counsels. The existence of such legislation means that the Church did not consider all men to be capable of entering the social religious state, and therefore the invitation to do so was not to be indiscriminately extended to all.

In the year 380, the Council of Saragossa prohibited clerics from embracing the monastic life "*propter luxum vanitatemque praesumptam*," (32) and the Council of Chalcedon (451) forbade the reception of a slave into the monastery in order to let him become a monk, unless there was previously granted the permission of his master. (33) A definite time of probation which candidates had to undergo was already determined by the V Council of Orleans (549), (34) and Pope Gregory the Great (590-604) explicitly legislated on several occasions concerning the admission of candidates into the religious state, prohibiting their reception into the monasteries of the Mediterranean because of the difficulty of the life, before they were eighteen years of age, (35) ordering the period of probation to last two years, (36) requiring for soldiers three years of probation and a very strict inquiry into their lives, (37) and prohibiting the reception of those who were bound by public office, (38) or who were married, unless the consort likewise entered the religious state. (39) The IV General Council of Constantinople

(32) C. 6—Bruns, II, 14; but cf. IV Council of Toledo (633), c. 50: "Clerici, qui monachorum propositum appetunt, quia meliorem vitam sequi cupiunt, liberos eis ab episcopo in monasteriis largiri oportet ingressus."—Bruns, I, 235. It has already been seen that the actual presence of a divine vocation, manifested at least through a right intention, has always been required by the Church in candidates for the religious state. Cf. *supra*, pp. 46-47.

(33) C. 4—Mansi, VII, 359.

(34) C. 19—Mansi, IX, 133.

(35) *Ep. 48* (ad Anthemium)—Mansi, IX, 1068; c. 6, X, *de regularibus et transeuntibus in religionem*, III, 31; JE, n. 1118.

(36) *Ep. 23* (ad Fortunatum Episcopum Neapolit.)—Mansi, X, 223; c. 6, C. XIX, q. 3; JE, n. 1776.

(37) *Ep. 11* (ad Eusebium, Urbicum, etc.)—Mansi, X, 92; c. 1, D. LIII; JE, n. 1497.

(38) *Loc. cit.*

(39) *Ep. 49* (ad Urbicum abbatem)—Mansi, X, 33

(869) demanded a three-year probation before the reception of the religious habit, allowing a shorter period in certain instances. (40)

The *Decree* of Gratian, besides giving attention to such impediments as non-age, (41) servitude, (42) the obligation of public affairs, (43) marriage (44) and the like, (45) also took up the question of the necessity of the period of probation before religious profession. The length of time required for the novitiate is found not to have been uniform for all: in one place the canons in the *Decretum* speak of a year, (46) in another, of two years, (47) and again, of three years, (48) which, as the *Glossa Ordinaria* intimated, could signify that the time for probation was optional and depended upon who was being received (a soldier, one who was unknown, etc.). (49) But some period of probation during which a prospective candidate could be tested was necessary for all, for as Rufinus (d.1190) said in commenting on *Causa* XVII:

> Quoniam quanto districtior est vita monachorum, tanto magis circa susceptionem monachalis habitus debet esse probationis experimentum, ideo exposcente ordinis ratione aliam seriem tractatus adjungit, ubi aperit, quomodo nullus debeat ingredi monasterium, nisi prius legitimo experimento probatus. (50)

Particularly after the IV Lateran Council (1215), when the religious state for the first time had its essential determinants fixed and clearly defined by the Church, and the ability to live in the common life and to contribute to the secondary ends of a particular institute became evident qualifications to be sought in *every* candidate for the religious state, was the probationary period before profession insisted upon. (51)

---

(40) C. 5—Mansi, XVI, 539.

(41) C. 1, C. XX, q. 1.

(42) C. 12, D. LIV.

(43) C. 1 D. LIII.

(44) Cc. 20, 21, 22, 23, C. XXVII, q. 2.

(45) A right intention also was required of the aspirant. A wrong intention was reflected in any material interest, provision for life, honor, dignities, etc. Cf. c. 20, C. XVI, q. 7; *dict.*, ante c. 1, D. LIII: "Quia frequenter, dum ab ecclesia repetuntur, plurima incommoda ecclesia sequitur, vel quia iidem curiales non voto religionis, sed ut offitiorum suorum ratiocinia fugiant, ad ecclesiam se transferunt;" cf. also Rufinus in *Die Summa Decretorum der Magister Rufinus* (ed. H. Singer, Paderborn, 1902), p. 136, who repeats the warning.

(46) C. 1, C. XVII, q. 2.

(47) C. 6, C. XIX, q. 3.

(48) C. 1, D. LIII; c. 3, C. XVII, q. 2.

(49) *Glossa ordinaria* ad c. 1, C. XVII, q. 2.

(50) *Op. cit.*, p. 371.

(51) The general legislation of the Church during this period, that is, from the IV Lateran Council to the Council of Trent, did not explicitly prescribe any new requirements in the candidate, but rather repeated and clarified the *ius antiquum* on the matter. The third book of the Decretals of Pope Gregory IX (1227-1241), titles 31 and 32, embraced practically all the former legislation and has always been a basis for books treating of entrance requirements for the religious state.

As Saint Bonaventure (1221-1274) wrote in commenting on the Rule of Saint Francis, it was expedient neither for the particular institute nor for the Church itself, that all who requested it be received without distinction. Not all men, he said, are able to sustain the rigors of the life, and the differences in quality and character of men being what they are, not everyone is a fit subject for community life, there being many who would disrupt the discipline of the institute and impede the progress of others. The results of indiscriminate acceptance, besides bringing discredit to the religious life generally, would only induce confusion and scandal into the Church itself. (52)

The novitiate, therefore, served a very practical and necessary purpose in this regard, for as Pope Innocent III (1198-1216) stated in a response to Ubaldus, Archbishop of Pisa, it was during this time that the institute was able to observe the candidate's fitness and to arrive at a decision whether or not he should be invited to make profession, and it also gave the candidate himself an opportunity to determine his own suitability for the religious life. (53) He decried the abuse of promoting candidates to profession before they had completed their novitiate, and while he acknowledged profession in such cases to be valid, he said the practice was to cease. (54) In 1244, Pope Innocent IV (1243-1254) ordered a full year of probation for Friars Preachers under the pain of invalidity of their subsequent profession. (55) Pope Alexander IV (1254-1261) extended the order to the Friars Minor, (56) and Pope Boniface VIII (1294-1303) applied it to all Mendicant Orders. (57)

b. From the Council of Trent to the Code of Canon Law

Tridentine legislation did not introduce any new note into the notion of religious vocation, but it did give force to the already existing concept: a vocation to the juridic religious state has its partial source in the invitation by a legitimate religious superior to a candidate who, after probation, is found qualified according to norms established by ecclesiastical legislation and approved Rule.

> Finito tempore novitiatus superiores novitios, quos habiles invenerint, ad profitendum admittent, aut e monasterio eos eiiciant. (58)

The mind of the Holy Synod on the point is quite clear: the religious state in its canonical development obviously is not the life for all: only the *habiles* are to be admitted, and no one is to be judged qualified before he has undergone at

---

(52) *Determin. quaest. circa Regulam S. Francisci*, pars I, quaes. 10, cited in Sleutjes, *Commentarius in Constitutiones Generales Fratres Minorum*, Vol. I (Ad Claras Aquas prope Florentiam, 1915), p. 23.

(53) C. 16, X, *de regularibus et transeuntibus in religionem*, III, 31; Potthast, n. 434.

(54) *Loc. cit.*

(55) Mansi, XXIII, 565-566; Potthast, n. 11416.

(56) C. 2, *de regularibus et transeuntibus ad religionem*, III, 14, in VI°.

(57) C. 3, *de regularibus et transeuntibus ad religionem*, III, 14, in VI°.

(58) Conc. Trident., sess. XXV, *de regularibus*, c. 16.

least a year's probation and has completed his sixteenth year, (59) thus being established the first general law setting up one complete year of novitiate as a necessary requisite for valid religious profession in institutes of both men and women.

No explicit mention was made by the Council of the nature of the qualifications to be possessed by the candidate; previous legislation and particularly the approved Rules of the individual institutes were to be the guiding norms in this matter. Indeed, when speaking of the religious profession of women, the Council expressly stated that if a candidate for a particular monastery freely and sincerely willed to embrace the religious life and was found to have the *qualifications required by the rule of that order*, and if the monastery was judged to be a suitable one for her, she could then be admitted to profession. (60) In other words, those were to be invited or called to profession who had been tested and found qualified according to norms which had been set up with a view not only to the individual's welfare but also that of the particular institute, and consequently of the religious state and of the Church itself. Those who, after examination, were not found to measure up to these standards, were to be dismissed as unsuited for the religious state, the ultimate decision in either case resting with the competent superior.

It was particularly in the post-Tridentine papal constitutions, however, that the nature and necessity of the ecclesiastical vocation found legal expression and the basic framework of a juridic religious vocation was established. To even the most casual observer, papal legislation following the Council of Trent clearly manifested the concern of the Roman Pontiffs that only the fit and qualified be allowed to assume the status of religious. Their instructions more than ever emphasized the fact that a juridic religious vocation is something very different from a simple call to perfection, and that the invitation to enter the *canonical* state of perfection had indeed become a very selective process. They ordered the exercise of a diligent watchfulness for the purpose of preventing disorder and decay from creeping into religious institutes, not a new concern of theirs to be sure. But in view of the ever increasing prominence of religious as official handmaids of the Church in its work of education, charity, etc., and the troubled times which followed the ravages of the Protestant Reformation, it is not surprising that their anxiety appears emphasized. And in no more noticeable way did their concern find expression than in legislation regarding the admission and rejection of candidates.

(59) "In quacumque religione tam virorum quam mulierum professio non fit ante decimum sextum annum expletum, nec qui minore tempore quam per annum post susceptum habitum in probatione steterit, ad professionem admittatur. Professio autem antea facta sit nulla, nullamque inducat obligationem ad alicuius regulae vel religionis vel ordinis observationem, aut ad alios quoscumque effectus."—Conc. Trident., sess. XXV, *de regularibus*, c. 15.

(60) Conc. Trident., sess. XXV, *de regularibus*, c. 17.

It was, for instance, out of solicitude for the preservation of the purity, integrity and dignity which are befitting to religious orders, and because of the respect which is due not only to the Divine Majesty, but also to persons consecrated to Him, that Pope Sixtus V (1585-1590) issued the Constitution *Cum de omnibus* on the 26th of November, 1587. (61) Prompted not only by the innate incongruity of persons offering themselves as holocausts to the omnipotent God when they had been repelled by the world because of their unsavory and sinful lives, but also by the consequent scandal and harm arising from the admission of such persons into institutes known to the world for their holy splendor and sanctity, (62) the Holy Father enacted stringent regulations concerning the admission of male candidates into the religious life. (63)

In the first place, because illegitimate children, he said, often were wont to imitate the vices of their parents and, in embracing the religious state for perverse motives, with their depraved morals and bad example not only harmed their associates in a particular institute, but also brought dishonor to all religious, (64) all illegitimate children of incestuous or sacrilegious unions were to be perpetually excluded from valid admission to the novitiate and profession. (65) Moreover, while other illegitimates (i.e., those not born of incest or sacrilege) might be allowed to enter religion, they first had to undergo careful scrutiny concerning their life, character, zeal, piety, integrity and learning, giving evidence that their virtues would compensate for the absence of legitimate birth, and their reception redound to the good of the entire institute. The judgment as to the suitability of these latter persons was to be made by the general or provincial superior with the unanimous consent of the chapter, and the violation of these prescriptions entailed the most severe penalties. (66)

The following year Pope Sixtus declared that such as became legitimated through the subsequent marriage of their parents were not to be included in his prohibition, (67) and Pope Gregory XIV (1590-1591) mitigated the law of his

---

(61) *Fontes*, n. 162.

(62) Preamble, *loc. cit.*

(63) The fact that the prescriptions of this Constitution apply to male religious only, and to clear up any doubts on the matter this was explicitly stated in his Constitution *Ad Romanum* of the following year (cf. n. 18—*Fontes*, n. 164), is not of great importance here. If such regulations had been needed for women at that time, they undoubtedly would have been given. The important point is that the canonical state of perfection which is made up of men *and* women must be preserved in its purity, integrity and dignity, and whenever legislation is needed to preserve it so, legislation shall be enacted. The laws of the Church are not mere whims; they are the result of its experience, and the prescriptions of this Constitution, as well as of others, are indicative of the state of affairs existing at the time.

(64) *Ibidem*, §1.

(65) *Ibidem*, §2.

(66) *Ibidem*, §3.

(67) Const. *Ad Romanum*, 21 oct. 1588, §3—*Fontes*, n. 164.

predecessor by permitting the reception of all illegitimate children, with the provision, however, that they were not to be admitted into an institute in which their father, either before or after their birth, had been professed, the prohibition remaining in force as long as the father lived. He nevertheless insisted on the same careful examination of such candidates as it had been ordered by Pope Sixtus. (68) A few years later Pope Clement VIII (1592-1605) still further tempered the law on illegitimacy as hindering entrance into the religious state by declaring that impediments set up by ecclesiastical law would no longer invalidate profession, but he ordered them to be observed by superiors under pain of falling into the penalties for non-compliance as enacted in the previous Constitutions. (69) The tenor of this legislation concerning the admission of illegitimates into the canonical state of perfection gives rise to the following impression: it was not the intention of the Holy See to prevent well-intentioned aspirants from embracing the religious state *when these could do so without bringing dishonor to that state or interfering with the work of its institutes.* However, the canonical state of perfection being what it was, namely, a public ecclesiastical state that entailed all the consequences of the common life, this latter consideration was of prime importance. Therefore, even though an individual, when prompted by grace did well to offer himself to religion, it could happen that because of circumstances over which he has no control, e.g., illegitimacy, he had to be refused admission and thus was denied the call to profession, though he certainly was not forbidden to pursue perfection on his own. The welfare of the whole religious state had to be considered, and, when it was necessary the individual had to give way to the common good. Laws enacted on such matters as touched illegitimacy, therefore, were intensified or mitigated not only according as the good of the individual may have demanded, but with due regard also to the welfare and the work of the religious state itself.

This was even more pointedly highlighted in the legislation dealing with criminals and persons suspected of grave crimes, and persons burdened with great debt. Pope Sixtus V, in his Constitution *Cum de omnibus*, perpetually excluded from the religious state all who were guilty or suspected of murder, of theft, of robbery and of similar crimes, as well as those who were in debt. Of particular importance to the interests of this study are the reasons advanced for these regulations. The Pontiff considered the enacted prescriptions to be absolutely necessary for two main reasons. Firstly, he said that it was a fact of experience that many men in trying to escape their deserved punishments and responsibilities in the world, offered themselves to the religious life without even the semblance of a right intention; they simply wished to hide and accordingly sought refuge behind the habit and the name of religion. Manifestly

(68) Cons. *Circumspecta*, 15 mart. 1591, §3—*Fontes*, n. 170.
(69) Cons. *In suprema*, 2 apr. 1602, §§3-4—*Bull. Rom. Taur.*, X, 768-769.

insincere, they obviously were offering a tremendous affront to Almighty God. In addition, however, besides disturbing the tranquility of those noble souls in the religious life who with a holy vocation were attempting to serve God, the admission of these irresponsible and evil men occasioned great opprobrium for the religious institute itself and was a source of scandal to many. (70) That is why, in all probability, the Holy Father at first made no provision for the admission of those who had reformed and thereupon became desirous of embracing the religious state from the purest of motives. He would have rejoiced to be the first to praise their conversion of morals, but with the good of the entire religious state in mind he apparently thought the danger of scandal too great in the wake of their admission to the religious life.

That it *was* the point of scandal which gave the greatest cause for concern in this matter is evidenced by the Pope's clarifying statement in the Constitution *Ad Romanum* the following year:

> Contra criminosos vero, quorum professio eadem Constitutione nostra irrita declaratur, ac propterea Iudicibus, et Curiis saecularibus procedendi facultas conceditur, tunc demum id locum habere volumus, et non aliter, cum actis publicis constiterit ipsos Iudices, et Curiam saecularem ante susceptionem habitus de ipso crimine adversus eos accusationem suscepisse, vel inquisitionem instituisse. (71)

Suarez in commenting on this legislation of Pope Sixtus, pointed out that purely occult crimes did not therefore make a person ineligible for the religious life. The act of the criminal had to be notorious in law as well as in fact, i.e., there had to be a *public* accusation of a particular individual with specific reference to the crime committed, and a *public* investigation of his guilt, for which *public* documents must have been drawn up. Even though a public but general investigation of the crime was held, if the identity of the perpetrator remained unknown, he was still eligible to enter the religious state. But, on the other hand, even if the one publicly accused and investigated was *de facto* innocent, the very fact that he was under suspicion and liable to prosecution debarred him from admission until his innocence stood proved in court. (72)

If according to Pope Sixtus, therefore, not the mere commission of a crime debarred one from validly and licitly embracing the religious state (a true repentance having meanwhile followed), but only the fact of public notoriety, then it must have been the prevention of the scandal that normally arose from such notoriety that was evidently uppermost in his mind. It was the good of the religious state which needed first to be considered, and for the insurance of its welfare every necessary legal precaution had to be taken. A vocation to

---

(70) Const. *Cum de omnibus*, 26 nov. 1587, §§4-5—*Fontes*, n. 162.

(71) Cons. *Ad Romanum*, 21 oct. 1588, §17—*Fontes*, n. 164.

(72) *De Religione*, tr. 7, lib. 5, c. 7, nn. 16-19; Vol. XV, pp. 328-329; also Reiffenstuel (1642-1703), *Ius Canonicum Universum* (5 vols. in 6, Romae, 1831-1834), lib. III, tit. 31, nn 79-80; Schmalzgrueber, *Ius Ecclesiasticum*, lib. III, tit. 31, n. 26.

the juridic religious state embraced much more than the individual's call to perfection by Almighty God; this state was to be made available for only those whom ecclesiastical authority had judged to be qualified according to norms it had juridically set up with the good of the entire religious state in view.

To guarantee the fulfillment of his prescriptions and the attainment of the ends for which he had enacted them, Pope Sixtus ordained the careful examination of every candidate for the religious life, the definitive judgment as to his fitness to be made by the superior general or the provincial superior, with the consent of the general or provincial chapter, as the case might call for. The judgment was to be based on accurate and trustworthy information regarding not only his freedom from crime and from any suspicion of crime, but concerning also his parents, nationality, past life, character and motives for entering the religious state, (73) and Pope Clement VIII on several occasions (74) warned superiors of their obligations in carrying out these prescriptions.

With ever increasing frequency and detail, legislation emanating from the Holy See during the following years continued to stress the need for the care which legitimate authority had to exercise in admitting only suitable aspirants to the religious state, (75) and although the laws indeed had in view not only

(73) Const. *Cum de omnibus*, nov. 26, 1587, §§4, 5, 6—*Fontes*, n. 162.

(74) Cf. const. *In suprema*, 2 apr. 1602, §§3, 4—*Bull. Rom. Taur.*, X, 768-769, and const. *Cum ad Regularem*, 19 mart. 1603—*Fontes*, n. 189.

(75) For the sake of exactness it should be noted that, apart from a specific designation of its intent to that effect, the general legislation that affected the religious state did not in and of its very nature (*per se*) apply to institutes of simple vows which, even after official recognition given them as enjoying the canonical state of perfection, did not become an integral part of the religious state in its juridic sense until the present Code of Canon Law (cf. *supra*, pp. 28-29). This has even greater application with regard to institutes of diocesan approval, established and existing by the sole will of the bishop (cf. Leo XIII, const. *Conditae a Christo*, 8 dec. 1900—*Fontes*, n. 644) until the year 1906, when episcopal rights in this matter were somewhat modified (cf. Pius X, motu propr. *Dei providentis*, 16 iul. 1906, §1—*ASS*, XXXIX (1906), 345). This fact did not, as it does not today, however, exclude such general legislation from being at least a directive norm which bishops could well impose on societies under their jurisdiction. It was the mind of the Holy See during this period—and it has not changed—that even institutes of diocesan approval be directed by the general regulations for the religious state, not indeed in the sense that they always constituted strict laws for institutes of diocesan approval, but that the Ordinaries were at least to endeavor to conform all institutes as far as possible to the government of religious societies in the strict sense: "Haec igitur Sacra Congregatio Negotiis Religiosorum Sodalium praeposita, summopere commendat Revmis locorum Ordinariis eorumque Delegatis seu Deputatis ad Monasteria, praesertim Monialium, quae Domum sui iuris constituunt, nec generalem Superiorissam habent, ut notitiam Decretorum, etiam in posterum edendorum, quae vitam religiosam respiciunt, effaciter evulgent inter Religiosas Familias et Instituta quoque Diocesana, ad abusus, si qui irrepserint, tollendos, ad bonum largius diffundendum et uniformitatem in rerum canonicarum observantiam ubique obtinendam."—S.C. de Religiosis, decr. *Apostolica Sedes*, 3 iul. 1910—*Fontes*, n. 4404; cf. also Wernz, *Ius Decretalium*, III, n. 628, note (222); Vermeersch, "Annotationes", *Periodica*, V (1913), 99, n. 3. Therefore it makes little differ-

the best interests of the individual seeking perfection but also the respect and honor which is owed to Almighty God, they manifested an even greater concern over the welfare of the religious state and the Church themselves, since this welfare was so intimately connected with the quality of the personnel that made up that state. While the limitations of space do not permit an examination of all of this legislation (which confirms rather than extends the concept already derived), the decree *Regulari disciplinae*, issued by the Sacred Congregation *Super Statu Regularium* on January 25, 1848, deserves special mention for its concise and explicit summation of the essential elements which have been emphasized in this study as constituting the basic framework of the juridic concept of religious vocation.

It is the greatest of care, so the decree stated, that must be exercised in the admission of aspirants to the religious state, *for nothing is more important to the welfare of that state.* Only those candidates were to be accepted (*ii tantum recipiantur . . . eos tantum probent*) who were endowed with the right intention, and who sought their personal sanctification (*cupientes Deo inservire, mundi pericula evitare*) *and* the good of their neighbor (*spirituali proximorum saluti qua exemplo, qua opere ad praescriptum Instituti, quod profitentur, consulere*). The judgment as to the presence or absence of the qualifications demanded in an aspirant could not be left to the postulant himself. The matter was too grave for such a private decision, for upon that prudent decision rested the future welfare not only of the individual, but of the entire public religious state. It was to be rendered, therefore, by men who were authoritative representatives of that state, and who were themselves outstanding in the qualities sought in the candidate, and it was to be rendered only after a most thorough examination and scrutiny of the subject (*ut eorum, qui religiosae familiae nomen daturi sint, indolem, ingenium, mores, ceterasque necessarias dotes accurate explorent, et sedulo investigent, quo consilio, quo spiritu, qua ratione ad regularem vitam ineundam ducantur*). (76)

Of special note also was the innovation which in the matter of accepting male postulants into the religious state was introduced by Pope Pius IX. From the time of the Constitution *Cum de omnibus* of Pope Sixtus V, the form of admitting candidates and the strict inquiry as to their qualifications and previous life had been minutely determined for religious superiors, but all this had been done

ence to the end of this study whether the legislation was directly enacted for institutes of solemn vows, or for those of simple vows, or both, as long as it refers simply to the canonical state of perfection. All such legislation, and particularly the purposes for which it was given, constituted the basic material out of which the synthetic concept of religious vocation could be drawn; for the congregations of simple vows were eventually to become incorporated in the juridic state of religious perfection and even the so-called "quasi-religious" and Secular Institutes can now by analogy be included in this concept.

(76) Preamble—*Fontes*, n. 4376. While the decree contains particular legislation only, having been addressed to religious institutes in Italy and its adjacent islands, this preamble patently was applicable to all institutes that harbored the canonical state of perfection.

without the enlisting of any aid from local Ordinaries. This omission had evidently proved unsatisfactory, for Pope Pius in his decree *Romani Pontifices*, issued through the Sacred Congregation *Super Statu Regularium* on January 25, 1848, ordered that thenceforth no male aspirant to the religious life was to be admitted without testimonial letters both from the Ordinary of his place of origin and also from the Ordinary of any place where he had spent more than one year after becoming fifteen years of age. A careful inquiry was to be made through these Ordinaries concerning all those matters to which previous legislation had adverted as items a knowledge of which was essential for superiors competent to admit candidates, and it was required to transmit this information to the proper superiors, who in turn were bound under severe penalties to ask for it. (77)

It is to be noted that the actual faculty of accepting a candidate for the religious state was not thereby made a prerogative of the bishop, but still remained within the competence of the legitimate religious superior. (78) By this new prescription, however, general ecclesiastical legislation for the first time sought the intervention of local ordinaries (and through them, of pastors, parochial assistants, and others upon whom ordinaries would naturally call for assistance) in the matter of determining who was to be called to the religious state and who was not to be called. (79) Later instructions from the Holy See modified and explained the decree minutely. (80)

---

(77) Nn. I, II, III—*Fontes*, n. 4375.

(78) But cf. Leo XIII, const. *Conditae a Christo*, 8 dec. 1900, c. 1, n. VII—*Fontes*, n. 644, where the bishop is given the faculty to admit women into diocesan congregations.

(79) Strictly taken, admission into the religious state is not had until actual profession, whether simple or solemn, by which act one is definitely and perpetually (at least virtually) incorporated in the state. As has been indicated, especially in the first part of this study, the novitiate is essentially the period of probation during which an aspirant's fitness for this actual call to the religious life is authoritatively adjudged by those competent to do so. But since the judgment has already begun in the act of admitting or rejecting a candidate for the novitiate itself, this latter act is at least remotely bound up with the juridical vocation in the strict sense, given at the time of profession. Cf. Wernz-Vidal, *De Religiosis*, p. 191.

Also indicated in the preceding pages is the fact that, until the Code of Canon Law, there was no uniform and constant practice in the determination of the superior who rendered the definitive judgment regarding a candidate's fitness for the novitiate and profession. With few exceptions, this was usually left to the prescriptions of particular rules (cf. *supra*, p. 75, note (29)). Even after ecclesiastical legislation had determined the matter on several occasions (cf., for example, Sixtus V, const. *Cum de omnibus*, 26 nov. 1587, §5—*Fontes*, n. 162; Leo XIII, const. *Conditae a Christo*, 8 dec. 1900, c. I, n. 7; c. II, n. 1—*Fontes*, n. 644), changes were often made with the approval of Rules and constitutions proper to orders and congregations.

(80) Cf. S. Congregatio super Statu Regularium, decr., 1 maii 1851; Leo XIII, litt. ap. *Orientalium*, 30 nov. 1848, n. X—*Fontes*, n. 627. Testimonials in the sense explained have never been required for women of the Latin rite. Ever since the Council of Trent, however, the bishop or his representative must examine every female candidate for the religious state,

Article III. Ecclesiastical Vocation to the Religious State and the Code of Canon Law

The elements which have been seen to form the traditional juridic concept of religious vocation are found contained, specified and sometimes modified, in the Code of Canon Law, but the concept itself has remained the same. No matter how absolutely certain anyone may be that it is God's will for him to enter the religious state, that life is closed to him unless an authorized superior, having used the legally established means to acquire the knowledge upon which his judgment is based, decides that the candidate, tried and proven, is qualified according to canonical norms, (81) and officially invites him to make his religious profession in a recognized institute. With that invitation he has the ecclesiastical vocation, he is morally certain (granted of course his actual sincerity) of the divine call, since the former may not be given by the superior unless he has evidence of the latter, manifested at least by a right intention, (82) and thus he truly has received a religious vocation. Without the ecclesiastical call, however, not only is it impossible for one to become a member of the canonical state of religious perfection, but to pass oneself off as such is nothing less than a usurpation. The Church, being the source of the very existence of the juridic religious state, has the sole prerogative to determine who will represent it in that mode of life, and the detrimental effects upon religion in general and a lessening of the Church's spiritual prestige whenever unsuited candidates are received into the religious state underscore the justification of its insistence upon careful discrimination in the matter.

The very phrasing of canon 538 clearly evinces the Church's recognition of its right, for it states that "Any Catholic who is not debarred by a legitimate impediment, and is prompted by a right intention, and is fitted for bearing the burdens of the religious life *may be admitted* (*admitti potest:* possible admission) into the religious state," and not that he *must be admitted* (*admitti debet:* mandatory admission) or that he is able to enter (*ingredi potest:* vested right of entry). In other words, no one has a strict right to enter a religious institute even on the grounds that he is free from impediments and is led by a right intention, and this no matter how holy that intention or how urgent his desires. Pope Pius X, as has been noted, explicitly sanctioned this truth in regard to the sacerdotal

---

both before her entrance into the novitiate and again before her profession of vows, to make certain that the applicant is acting with full knowledge and full liberty. Cf. sess. XXV, *de regularibus*, c. 17; cf. also Pius V, const. *Etsi mendicantium*, 16 maii 1567, §1, n. 6; §2, n. 6—*Fontes*, n. 121; Leo XIII, const. *Conditae a Christo*, 8 dec. 1900, §1, n. VIII—*Fontes*, n. 644; can. 552, §2.

(81) What these norms are at the present time shall be briefly seen in the following chapter, where they are viewed as the essential conditions and sufficient signs of a religious vocation today.

(82) Cf. *supra*, pp. 58-59.

state, (83) and what he affirmed of the priesthood holds just as well for the religious state. (84) There is one distinction to be made, however. From the divine constitution of the ecclesiastical hierarchy and the form of rule in the Church, a divine-human society, it follows that ecclesiastical acceptance for the priesthood is necessary by divine law, (85) but it is only by human law, the source of the presently existing religious state, that there is demanded today an acceptance of candidates into that state. Nevertheless the fact remains that the ecclesiastical vocation *is* necessary for both.

The present law of the Church gives the right of admitting candidates to the novitiate and to subsequent profession, either temporary or perpetual, to major religious superiors (86) after they have taken the vote of the council or of the chapter, according as the particular constitutions of each order or congregation prescribe. (87) In virtue of canon 575, the vote of the council or the chapter is decisive in the admission to the first vows after the novitiate, and merely consultive for the subsequent perpetual profession of either simple or solemn vows. (88) As the Code does not determine the force of the vote as regards admission

(83) Litterae ex Secretariae Status, 1 iul. 1912: "Neminem habere unquam ius ullum ad ordinationem antecedenter ad liberam electionem episcopi."—*AAS*, IV (1912), 485.

(84) This is the common opinion among authors. Cf. Coronata, *Institutiones*, I, 704, note (2); Vermeersch, "Annotationes", *Periodica*, VI-VII (1912-1914), 263-265; Blat, *Commentarium*, Vol. II, Pars II et III, p. 269. But cf. Woywod, *Commentary*, I, 240: "The right which the Code gives to every Catholic under the above conditions (i.e., those listed in canon 538) entails an obligation for the religious organization to which a candidate applies to receive him or her. If a candidate possess the proper qualifications fot the respective community, and is able and willing to comply with the conditions for admission as they are determined by the constitutions of the community, it is morally wrong to refuse admission." The present writer agrees that a moral wrong might, under certain circumstances, be committed, e.g., against charity, but, in view of what has been seen, denies that the wrong would constitute a violation of strict justice.

(85) Cf. Carr, *Vocation to the Priesthood*, pp. 30-32.

(86) Local religious superiors (except the superior of an independent monastery) are minor superiors; all other superiors (provincial, superior general, etc.) are major. Cf. Bouscaren-Ellis, *Commentary*, pp. 239-240. Since local ordinaries are never called major superiors in the Code, their former right of admitting candidates to the novitiate in diocesan congregations (cf. Leo XIII, const. *Conditae a Christo*, 8 dec. 1900, c. 1, n. VII—*Fontes*, n. 644) has been abrogated. They need a special mandate from the Holy See to do so. Cf. Beste, *Introductio*, p. 369; Woywod, *Commentary*, I, 247; Coronata, *Institutiones*, I, 717; Creusen-Garesché-Ellis, *Religious Men and Women*, p. 139; Schaefer, *De Religiosis*, p. 450.

(87) Can. 543.

(88) Whenever the law requires a superior to seek the consent or counsel of some persons before acting, if consent is required, any action taken by the superior contrary to the vote of these persons is invalid; if consultation only is demanded, it suffices for the validity of the action if the superior consults the persons specified, and he is not strictly obliged to follow their vote even if it be unanimous. Cf. canon 105, 1°. The canon's phrase, "satis est ad valide agendum ut Superior illas personas audiat," when consultation only is required, is admittedly obscure. Bouscaren-Ellis (*Commentary*, p. 91) cite Vermeersch-Creusen, Van

into the novitiate, the particular constitutions may rule whether the vote is to be decisive or only consultive in that case. (89)

It is the juridic act of the proper superior admitting the candidate to his first profession, however, that precisely comprises the ecclesiastical vocation to the religious state, (90) for it is by this profession that one becomes a religious in the strict sense. (91) While it is indeed true, as Coronata points out, (92) that the right of admitting a candidate to first profession does not pertain to the superior alone, but to the superior *with the consent* of the council or chapter, it is also a fact, recognized by the same author (93) among others, (94) that canons 543 and 572, §1, 2°, give the actual power of admitting or rejecting a candidate to the major superior and *not* to the council or chapter. This is not really a contradiction, for even though that body of councilors unanimously decides to admit a candidate, the superior is not bound to do so and may refuse him. In other words, it is the proper superior himself who in the last analysis actually gives or refuses the ecclesiastical call to the religious state, although he may not *give* it without the consent of his advisers. The point is a minor one, however, as far as the purpose of this study is concerned. The important thing is that it is the Church, a public moral person, in its nature of a supreme and sovereign society, that is bringing its powers to bear through the medium of duly constituted representatives, and giving the call. (95)

But while the superior's definitive act of selecting a candidate for profession is the result of a judgment made with the aid of his council or chapter, in practice much that is preambulatory and directive of that choice rests within the discretion of others, especially of the novice master. The traditional period of

---

Hove, Boudinhon and Vidal as holding that the counsel is not a requisite for valid action, and Maroto, Ojetti, Ferreres and Coronata as saying that the counsel is a requisite for validity. It is a clear case of a *dubium iuris*, and therefore, until an authentic interpretation is given on the matter, the principles of canon 15 have place here, and the admission of a candidate to *perpetual* profession by a major superior without the advice required by law may certainly be regarded as valid.

(89) Creusen-Garesché-Ellis (*op. cit.*, p. 139) think that canon 543 implies that it is a decisive vote, but admit that grave authorities allow the constitutions to decide on the matter, and place this question also in the category of a *dubium iuris*.

(90) This act of judgment regarding a candidate's suitability and the invitation to profession is not, of course, to be confused with the prescript of canon 572, §1, 6°, that the profession *shall be received* by the lawful superior according to the constitutions, either personally or by his representative. The two acts are altogether distinct; it is only the first that comprises "the call."

(91) Cf. *supra*, p. 85, note (79).

(92) *Institutiones*, I, 716.

(93) *Ibidem*, p. 717.

(94) Cf., e.g., Beste, *Introductio*, p. 368.

(95) Actually, of course, as Wernz-Vidal note, the right of admitting candidates into the religious state resides principally in the Roman Pontiff, who ordinarily does not exercise it himself. Cf. *De Religiosis*, p. 215, note (1).

probation before profession, when a candidate's suitability for the religious state is carefully observed while he is being instructed in the way of perfection, (96) continues to be, under the law of the Code, one complete year in institutes of both men and women. (97) During this time the formation of the novices and the direction of the novitiate belong exclusively to the master of novices, and no one may interfere under any pretext whatsoever (except superiors in cases provided for by the constitutions). (98) He and his assistant are even freed from all occupations which could in any way hinder them in the care and guidance of their charges. (99)

No one, therefore, should be better able to judge regarding a candidate's suitability for the religious state than the novice master, and particularly so since he is the only professed member of the community who is allowed contact with him. (100) Towards the end of the novitiate, guided by the demands of canon law and of the particular constitutions, he makes known to the lawful superiors his judgment that the subject either has or has not fulfilled all the necessary requirements, and does or does not possess all the qualifications for first profession. (101) As can readily be seen, therefore, the novice master plays no small role in the granting of the ecclesiastical vocation, even though it is the major superior who actually gives the call.

Other factors, of course, also have place in influencing the judgment of the superior. Even before the probation of the novitiate, in institutes with perpetual vows all the women and, in institutes of men, the lay brothers (102) must make a "postulancy" of at least six whole months. (103) This term denotes a period of preparation and testing preliminary to the probation, properly so-called, of the novitiate itself, during which time a candidate is given the opportunity to

(96) Can. 565, §1: Annus novitiatus debet sub disciplina Magistri hoc habere propositum, ut informetur alumni animus studio regulae et constitutionum, piis meditationibus assiduaque prece, iis perdiscendis quae ad vota et ad virtutes pertinent, exercitationibus opportunis ad vitiorum semina radicitus extirpanda, ad compescendos animi motus, ad virtutes acquirendas.

(97) Can. 555, §1, 2°. This is the so-called "canonical year" of novitiate and is a necessary requisite for valid profession in every religious institute. If approved particular constitutions require a second or even a third year of novitiate, the prescripts of these constitutions naturally must be observed.

(98) Can. 561, §1.

(99) Can. 559, §3.

(100) Can. 564.—§1: Novitiatus ab ea parte domus, in qua degunt professi, sit, quantum fieri potest, segregatus ita ut, sine speciali causa ac Superioris vel Magistri licentia, novitii nullum habeant communicationem cum professis, neque hi cum novitiis.

(101) Can. 563.

(102) That is, lay religious devoted exclusively to manual labor; hence not all religious professed as brothers in a religious institute are lay brothers, *conversi*, in the canonical sense. Cf. Bouscaren-Ellis, *Commentary*, p. 258.

(103) Can. 539, §1. "In institutes with temporary vows the prescriptions of the constitutions regarding the necessity and duration of the postulancy are to be followed."—*Loc. cit.*

become acquainted with the nature and the obligations of the religious life, and superiors are able to judge on the evidences of the aptitudes and dispositions which entitle the subject to the real test of his vocation in the novitiate. Since the purpose of the postulancy is essentially the same as that of the novitiate, (104) to furnish a means of judgment as to the candidate's suitability for the religious state, it is, so to speak, an integral part of the ecclesiastical call to the religious state. It definitely is an important step towards that goal. And inasmuch as postulants can be placed under the care of an experienced religious other than the novice master, (105) the opinion of yet another individual may thus play an important role in the granting of that call. (106)

The testimonial letters required by the Code before entrance into the novitiate are also an important source of information upon which the definitive decision of the proper superiors is based, especially since the Code has suppressed certain impediments, even some which were of rather recent date, thus leaving much greater liberty to the judgment of superiors. All who are required by law to furnish these testimonials (107) are under a grave obligation to make known in them everything which concerns the character, conduct, reputation, and knowledge of the candidate, anything, in other words, which would have a

(104) Schaefer, *De Religiosis*, p. 413.

(105) Can. 540, §1: Postulatus peragi debet vel in domo novitiatus vel in alia religionis domo in qua disciplina secundum constitutiones accurate servetur sub speciali cura probati religiosi. Cf. Schaefer, *De Religiosis*, p. 419: "In Domo novitiatus Magister novitiorum vel eius Socius, cum sit vir magis idoneus, curam specialem pro postulantibus suscipere potest, in aliis Domibus alius probatus Religiosus."

(106) The prescriptions which relate to the postulancy, however, do not affect the validity of admission into the novitiate or of subsequent profession, though their violation in certain cases may constitute a grave fault. Cf. Creusen-Garesché-Ellis, *Religious Men and Women*, p. 132; Schaefer, *De Religiosis*, p. 415.

(107) Can. 544, §1: In quavis religione omnes adspirantes, antequam admittantur, exhibere devent testimonium recepti baptismatis et confirmationis.

§2: Adspirantes viri debent praeterea testimoniales litteras exhibere Ordinarii originis ac cuiusque loci in quo, post expletum decimum quartum aetatis annum, morati sint ultra annum moraliter continuum, sublato quolibet contrario privilegio.

§3: Si agatur de admittendis illis qui in Seminario, collegio vel alius religionis postulatu aut novitiatu fuerunt, requiruntur praeterea litterae testimoniales, datae pro diversis casibus a rectore Seminarii vel collegii, audito Ordinario loci, aut a maiore religionis Superiore.

§4: Pro clericis admittendis, praeter testimonium ordinationis, sufficiunt litterae testimoniales Ordinariorum in quorum dioecesibus post ordinationem ultra annum moraliter continuum sint commorati, salvo praescripto §3.

§5: Religioso professo, ad aliam religionem ex apostolico indulto transeunti, satis est testimonium Superioris maioris prioris religionis.

§6: Praeter haec testimonia a iure requisita, possunt Superiores, quibus ius est adspirantes in religionem cooptandi, alia quoque exigere, quae ipsis ad hunc finem necessaria aut opportuna videantur.

§7: Mulieres denique ne recipiantur, nisi praemissis accuratis investigationibus circa earum indolem et mores, firmo praescripto §3.

bearing on his admission into the religious state. (108) While the testimonial letters contain information, not direction, and the proper superiors will give the ultimate decision whether or not to admit a candidate, these letters nevertheless serve as an evident aid to these superiors in their judgment on the presence or the absence of the necessary conditions and sufficient signs of a religious vocation in a candidate, without whose favorable judgment and invitation to profession a religious vocation simply does not exist. (109)

(108) Cf. can. 545, §4.

(109) As has been stated previously, the concept of vocation to the other canonical states of perfection does not essentially differ from the religious vocation concept. In the admission of candidates, "*quasi-religious*" societies follow the prescripts of their own approved constitutions, subject to the laws of canon 542 on the qualifications needed for valid and licit entrance (cf. can. 677), and Secular Institutes are bound only by their own constitutions in the matter. But in neither case can one become a member of the canonical state of perfection if one is not officially invited by an authorized superior, who having in view not only the good of the individual, but also the welfare of the state and the Church, decides what he thinks best for all concerned.

CHAPTER VI

THE ESSENTIAL CONDITIONS AND THE SUFFICIENT SIGNS OF A RELIGIOUS VOCATION

Religious superiors are faced with a grave and twofold responsibility in selecting candidates for the canonical state of perfection. They are first of all bound in charity not to reject unwarrantedly candidates who have responded to Christ's invitation to the higher life by heeding the Church's insistence that the surest and quickest way to perfection lies in the religious state, and they have a correlative obligation towards the Church not to refuse admittance to these worthy aspirants whose lives "in religion" contribute so much to its glory and welfare. (1) But at the same time they must exercise the greatest care that only fit and suitable subjects be allowed into the religious state which, as a public ecclesiastical state that entails all the consequences of the common life, has been seen to demand more of the aspirant than his good intentions alone. Quality must not be sacrificed for the sake of quantity, and this necessitates a prudent discrimination among the candidates for profession, a process which has its beginnings long before the definitive judgment given at the end of the novitiate.

This, of course, has been the burden of the preceding pages, and in those same pages has been stated the Church's succinctly phrased norm which superiors and their aids are to use as a guide in judging a candidate's suitability for the presently existing religious state:

(1) This latter obligation is usually expressed as "the Church's need for vocations," a phrase never before voiced so much as in the present day. In recent years many "Institutes" have been held to promote zeal and techniques for discovering and developing vocations, the proceedings of many of which have been published and may be read with profit, and today's great need for vocations both to the priesthood and to the religious state has been constantly reiterated by the participants.

The present writer finds it significant as well as interesting that while the primary end of the religious state (self-perfection) is not at all forgotten in the discussions which are held in these institutes, the emphasis on the present need for religious vocations is seen to rise out of the corresponding need for men and women to serve the Church in the fields of education, charity, social service and other apostolic activities. Likewise, unofficial but reliable reports on the unprecedented congress of all male institutes of perfection in the Church, recently held in Rome (November-December, 1950) under the auspices of the Sacred Congregation of Religious, relate that much attention was given in the discussions as to how the secondary ends of the religious state might be further adapted to meet the changed conditions of the world short of interference with the basic structure of the religious life. All of this serves to underline the emphasis which this study has placed on the present nature of the juridic religious state as a most important social arm of the Church as well as *the school* of perfection.

In religionem admitti potest quilibet catholicus qui nullo legitimo impedimento detineatur rectaque intentione moveatur, et ad religionis onera ferenda sit idoneus. (2)

In this statement, as has been noted, is contained the Church's explicit summation of the essential conditions and sufficient signs of a religious vocation. A superior's prudent judgment, in other words, is to be guided by the objective reality of law, not by subjective projection: he cannot accept less than what the law demands, nor can he require more. It but remains, therefore, to examine this norm in so far as it falls within the scope of this study.

But first there is need of an important observation. It is said that canon 538 is to be examined "in so far as it falls within the scope of this study." In other words, the mere statement of the law and its *canonical* commentary is not the whole of the story of vocation, a point which was emphasized at the very outset of this work. What follows is not presented as a substitute for the valuable and necessary theological and ascetical works on religious vocation; it is seen rather as the legislator's basic guide for the latter, the bounds within which the theologian and spiritual director work. The explicit statement of the law and its necessary implications in the light of what has already been seen are emphasized here, but by no means is this emphasis to be construed as relegating theological concepts to a subordinate place in the matter of religious vocation. On the contrary, to recall the fundamental position taken in this study: the total concept of vocation to the religious state can be had only when the cognate theories of law and theology which go to form that concept are seen in proper relation one to the other, each receiving its due emphasis, each viewed in context, in the totality of which it forms a part. (3)

Article I. Some Fundamental Specifications of Canon 538

As has been noted, the essential qualifications demanded in candidates for the religious state have not remained fixed and static in all ages or in all localities. While it is true that the basic norms of morality and goodness are absolute, and that the effective realization of the religious state's vast potentiality for good in the world will always depend upon the presence of certain fundamental qualities in its adherents, it is also a fact, well substantiated in history, that some requirements which seem so necessary for religious in one age or locality will be of less import in another, and perhaps of no consequence at all in yet others. (4) It follows, therefore, that one and the same individual might be a qualified candidate for the religious state, or have a religious vocation, one year but not the next, *the difference resulting from a change, not in the candidate, but in the law itself.*

Canon 538 allows for just such vicissitudes by simply prohibiting admission into the religious state to anyone who is bound by a legitimate impediment,

(2) Can. 538.

(3) Cf. *supra*, pp. 1-3.

(4) Cf. *supra*, pp. 69-70, 80-83.

canon 542 going on to specify what these impediments are *by general law at the present time.* (5) Although it is highly improbable that *all* of the impediments of canon 542 will some day be abrogated, (6) not to mention the absolute permanence of the impediments of the natural law, such as insanity and grave nervous disorders generally, (7) in view of past history and the anticipated changes in the world of the future, it is at least possible that *some* of them will one day cease to exist, while on the other hand future candidates for the religious state might well be bound by other impediments not in force today. This contingency will depend upon legitimate authority setting up those impediments which at the time will be seen to be necessary for the good of the individual, the religious state, society, and the Church. They need not be immutably constant, and probably will not be.

In addition it should be noted that ecclesiastical impediments of both the general and the particular law can be dispensed from, the Holy See alone dispensing from the former, while the approved constitutions of pontifical institutes usually grant superiors general the power to dispense from impediments of the particular law, local ordinaries by the very nature of things being competent to grant dispensations from the impediments enacted in the constitutions of diocesan congregations. (8) The presence of an impediment admitting of dispensation, therefore, does not necessarily create a presumption against a *possible* vocation to the religious life. Each case must be considered individually, and if all the other qualifications of the candidate be of such a nature as to warrant a petition for a dispensation, (9) the presence of a vocation might rightfully be indicated, and if the petition is granted and all other necessary conditions have been fulfilled, then the ecclesiastical call may validly and lawfully be given. (10) These facts serve to point up the role of ecclesiastical law and authority in the matter of religious vocation, and emphasize the necessity for spiritual directors in general and religious superiors in particular to be cognizant of the law as well as of the principles of theology in determining its presence.

---

(5) A complete listing of these impediments will be given in the following article.

(6) Certainly not such impediments which make entrance into the religious state invalid for those who are compelled by means of grave fear, deceit, or fraud, or who are admitted by a superior thus constrained, or who are married (for the duration of their marriage). Cf. can. 542, 1°.

(7) Coronata, *Institutiones*, I, p. 703; Wernz-Vidal, *De Religiosis*, p. 187; Schaefer, *De Religiosis*, pp. 408-409.

(8) Bouscaren-Ellis, *Commentary*, pp. 261-262. By virtue of their Quinquennial Faculties, local ordinaries in the United States also have the power to dispense from the particular impediments of illegitimacy and advanced age (not in excess of forty years) in so far as these impediments are enacted in the constitutions of *any* religious institute. Cf. Eagleton, *The Diocesan Quinquennial Faculties Formula IV*, The Catholic University of America Canon Law Studies, n. 248 (Washington, D. C.: The Catholic University of America Press, 1948), pp. 99-102, 105-107.

Of even more immediate consequence is the correlative fact that an individual might be a qualified candidate for membership in one religious institute but at the same time be unsuited, or lacking a vocation, to another. While it has been seen that the essential nature of the religious state has been established by law, it has also been observed that the law wisely makes ample provision for diversity among the various communities which make up that state, a diversity which has been characteristic of the religious life since its very inception, and exhibited not only in the variety of secondary pursuits proper to each institute, but also in uniqueness of spirit and manner of approach to the common goal of perfection. (11) The effect of such accidental divergencies upon entrance into the religious life is obvious and has already been indicated. To repeat: an admitting superior must not only judge the sincerity of a candidate's intention to follow the evangelical counsels, but in addition must ask himself whether or not, in *consideration of the positive constitution and the nature of his particular institute*, it is to the general interest of that society, as well as that of the individual, the religious state, and the Church, that *this individual* be admitted into *this specific institute*. Conditions of health, of character, of education, etc., which are not demanded by the evangelical counsels taken in themselves, or by another institute, might be a necessary prerequisite for the members of his community, and even certain particular impediments over and above those found in the general law might prohibit a candidate's entrance into it.

Canon 542 in including the prescripts found in particular constitutions (12) when specifying the "legitimate impediments" adverted to in canon 538, takes cognizance of this contingency, and in the light of the same reality must the latter canon's qualification, "*in religionem admitti potest . . .* (*qui*) *ad religionis onera ferenda sit idoneus*," be interpreted. In other words, to have a religious vocation an individual need not possess the requisites demanded by *every* religious community, but he must be qualified according to the norms of the general law and of at least *one* canonically recognized institute. The word "*idoneus*" in the context of canon 538, therefore, refers to one's suitability for the religious state

---

(9) A knowledge of the practice of the Holy See with respect to dispensations from religious impediments is of evident importance for religious superiors and vocation counselors. The impediment of marriage, for example, is very rarely dispensed from, and only in the case of elderly persons. Cf. Bouscaren-Ellis, *Commentary*, p. 260.

(10) It should be recalled that the presence of an impediment, either of the natural or the ecclesiastical law, which does not admit of dispensation, and which, through no fault of his own, prohibits a candidate from valid or lawful admission into the religious state, is a strong indication that he has not even received a *divine* religious vocation, and this no matter how fine and praiseworthy his intentions might be. Cf. *supra*, pp. 35, note (10), 57, note (107), 62.

(11) Cf. *supra*, pp. 26-29, 30, note (76), 70.

(12) In many institutes, for example, the admission of those who are illegitimate or who exceed a certain age is forbidden by particular law. Cf. Beste, *Introductio*, p. 364, note (4).

in general, in the sense that one who possesses the qualifications which are common to all institutes need not in addition be qualified for one specific institute and for that institute alone; but since the religious state actually exists in the form of concrete orders and congregations and not in the abstract, this suitability to be effective must also correspond to the requirements of at least one of these communities. Any other interpretation leaves the term without operative significance. (13)

Over and above the evident application which this fact has in causing superiors and vocational directors to keep in mind the particular demands of the specific institute an aspirant desires to enter in addition to the basic requirements of the religious life in general, there is another consideration to be acknowledged here, of no less importance but, as it seems, of some less manifest relevancy. It is this: the certainty that an individual is not a qualified subject for one community, whether because he is prohibited through the existence of an impediment of the particular law or because he lacks the aptitude for the special works of that institute, does not by that fact give rise to a like certainty that he has no religious vocation at all. Indeed, he may very well be a splendid candidate for any number of canonical institutes, and it seems to the writer that a superior, if he must by law refuse such a person admission into his own community, has yet an obligation in charity to direct him to these other institutes if he deems him qualified. And more than that: even granted that a particular individual in the judgment of the superior is an acceptable candidate for his community, it may very well happen that he might be even more suitable by temperament, talents, inclinations, etc., for another religious institute, and again it seems to the writer that the superior should direct this individual to the institute where he might better serve himself, the religious state as a whole, society, and the Church. Provincialism should have no place in the religious life and, indeed, is contrary to the law itself which holds up the entire religious state as an object of honor (14) and aptly provides for the diversity which has proved so beneficial to the Church. A provincial and parochial attitude, which would think in terms of a single community rather than in terms of the honor and

---

(13) The word "*idoneus*" as used in canon 538 has been variously interpreted by authors. Bouscaren-Ellis (*Commentary*, p. 258), for instance, equate it to the mental, moral and physical qualities necessary to bear the burdens and to fulfill the offices of the religious state in general, while Toso (*Ad Codicem Juris Canonici Commentaria Minora* [5 vols., Vol. I, 2. ed., 1921; Vols. II-V, 1922-1927, Romae: Marietti], V, 87) restricts its application to the narrower sense of suitability for the work of a particular institute in question. Blat's interpretation of the term as having reference both to the common requirements of the religious life in general and to some institute in particular, is in accord with that expressed above: "Legislator igitur praemittens normam generalem, utrumque debuit respicere, quidquam nempe omnibus religionibus commune sine diversitate ipsarum et aliud peculiare uniuscuisque religionis modo generali expressum."—*Commentarium*, II, Pars II et III, n. 282, p. 269.

(14) Can. 487.

glory of the religious state as a whole, can turn zeal for vocations into a contest for numbers, a phenomenon directly opposed to canon 538 and allied precepts of the Code, which patently do not seek quantity at the expense of quality in the religious state.

And lastly there is the basic and, to the writer, a most important consideration which arises from a correlation of canon 538 and canons 487, 488, 1°, 593, 562 and 565, §1. Concisely stated in canons 487, 488, 1°, and 593 is the law's summary of the essential nature and the end of the religious state, (15) matter treated at some length particularly in the first part of this study. (16) The religious state, it is once again emphasized, offers the best possible (but not the only) means of *striving for* perfection, and the employment of this verbal connotation, "striving for perfection", is pertinently exact: the state is one of perfection to be acquired (*status perfectionis acquirendae*), not one of perfection already acquired (*status perfectionis acquisitae*); (17) a candidate for the religious life, in other words, is not expected to have actually attained perfection before being eligible for admission. Canon 538 and allied legislation, therefore, which for the reasons sufficiently explained above require a definite standard of fitness in a person before he may be received into the canonical state of perfection, are not to be so strictly interpreted as to present an awe-inspiring obstacle in the path of well-intentioned and canonically qualified applicants, who usually are all too conscious of how far they have yet to go to fulfill Our Lord's desire that they be perfect as their Heavenly Father is perfect. (18) That goal has no limits and implies *all* the virtues working at their greatest intensity, something which is effected, with the help of grace, only through education, training and practice.

Therefore as canons 562 (19) and 565, §1, (20) imply, suitable subjects for the

(15) Can. 487: Status religiosus seu stabilis in communi vivendi modus, quo fideles, praeter communia praecepta, evangelica quoque consilia servanda per vota obedientiae, castitatis et paupertatis suscipiunt, ab omnibus in honore habendus est.

Can. 488, 1°: [Religio est] societas, a legitima ecclesiastica auctoritate approbata, in qua sodales, secundum proprias ipsius societatis leges, vota publica, perpetua vel temporaria, elapso tamen tempore renovanda, nuncupant, atque ita ad evangelicam perfectionem tendunt.

Can. 593: Omnes et singuli religiosi, Superiores aeque ac subditi, debent, non solum quae nuncuparunt vota fideliter integreque servare, sed etiam secundum regulas et constitutiones propriae religionis vitam componere atque ita ad perfectionem sui status contendere.

(16) Cf. *supra*, pp. 11-33.

(17) "Status perfectionis acquisitae est status Episcoporum, qui vi officii suscepti ad perfectionem sive caritatem exercendam obligantur; quadam ratione etiam sacerdotes, quos Episcopi in curam animarum assumunt, istius sunt."—Schaefer, *De Religiosis*, p. 50. For a comparison of the religious state, the episcopacy and the priesthood, cf. S. Thomas, *Summa Theologica*, Ia, IIae, q. 184, a. 6 and 8; q. 188, a. 6.

(18) Cf. St. Matthew, V, 48.

(19) "The master of novices is under grave obligation to exercise the utmost diligence in instructing the novices in the zealous practice of the religious life, according to the constitutions and the regulations of canon 565."

religious state can, with certain restrictions, be molded or, as Duffy so aptly phrases it, "we think it is a good policy for vocational counselors to look for *subjects for vocations* to the religious life, and not *subjects with vocations*." (21) Given the certain fundamental needs and basic attitudes desirable in prospective religious, the raw material with which to work, defects of character of whatever nature, perhaps even distressing complexes and emotional states of one sort or another, can in many cases be corrected through the system of the novitiate which, as canon 565, §1, states, undertakes the formation of subjects by steps and degrees through discipline, correction, observation, positive training, etc. (22) The novitiate is the special school " . . . where attitudes and dispositions of holiness are sown as seeds, where aptitudes are tested, habits of virtue set . . . ;" (23) it not only tests what is already present in the aspirant, in other words; it actually gives him something. It thus can happen, therefore, that one who once might have appeared to many as an unlikely prospect for the religious life, may so respond to expert guidance in the novitiate as to not only meet the minimum standards required for profession but, what is more important, give every indication that he will continue to progress in his chosen state in life, that of *acquiring* perfection.

Naturally, the "fundamental needs" and "basic attitudes," mentioned above as the "raw material" so important for such an accomplishment, cannot be dispensed with. To attempt to prepare an individual for the religious life if he is affected with a definite psychopathic or neurotic condition with incurable natural causes is to attempt more than can reasonably be expected. Abnormal persons definitely are not fit for the religious life; if a candidate is to profit from the training of the novitiate, he must have a fundamentally sound, harmonious, and well-balanced disposition of the faculties of the soul: his mind with its imagination, memory and judgment should not show any striking deviation from the normal. (24)

---

(20) "The purpose of the year of novitiate under the guidance of the master must be the formation of the novices' character by the study of the rules and constitutions, by pious meditations and assiduous prayer, by instructions in all matters pertaining to the vows and the cultivation of virtue, and by pious exercises conducive to the complete eradication of faulty habits, the control of the passions and the acquisition of virtues."

(21) *Testing the Spirit*, p. 14 (italics inserted).

(22) Progress in perfection should not, of course, cease at the end of the novitiate, but in the words of Pope Pius XI: "Let the novices never forget that the kind of men they are in the novitiate, the same they will be for the rest of their lives."—Ap. litt., *Unigenitus Dei Filius*, 19 mart. 1924 (*AAS*, XVI [1924], 142).

(23) Duffy, *op. cit.*, p. 30; cf. also *Religious Sisters* [An English translation by anonymous persons of *Directoire des Superieures* and *Les Adaptations de la Vie Religieuse*, papers read at the Journées d'Etudes and arranged by the editor of *La Vie Spirituelle*] (Westminster, Md.: Newman, 1950), 226 ff.

(24) Cf. Duffy, *op. cit.*, p. 19; the same author (pp. 86-87) quotes Saint Theresa of Avila to the effect that the religious life can do many wonderful things for a person, but it cannot

Another factor which is of considerable importance in this regard is the truth that years of habit make the correction of character traits extremely difficult. Wrong inner attitudes, deficient aptitudes, unwholesome emotional states, and like maladjustments, are not easily rectified in middle life, but only by proper direction and help in the time of youth. Obviously, therefore, the role of parents, teachers, the parish priest, the home, the school, the church, cannot be underestimated when it comes to "the fostering of religious vocations." The proper training of the youth has an evident and direct connection with the reality of his vocation and, it need hardly be said, it is particularly the good Catholic home in which vocations are planted, take root and grow: it is there that is begun the tuition, the education, the formation of the subject in proper motives, values, good purposes, and real ends of effort. And such early training has special consequences in the matter of a vocation to the religious state which, in view of its present particular nature and needs, can neither afford too long a time for the basic religious formation of the candidate nor permit that disciplining to interfere with the progress of others in a community.

The essential conditions and the sufficient signs of a religious vocation as defined in canon 538, therefore, are to be viewed in the light of the meaning and implications of canon 487, 488, 1°, and 593, which present that state as a *school* of perfection as well as an important social arm of the Church, and canons 562 and 565, §1, which speak of the training of subjects *for* vocation. These considerations must find place in all theological systems on grace, predestination and free will, and *a fortiori*, therefore, in all concepts of divine vocation, although *in theory* they will be variously interpreted by the different systems. But to state once more the burden of this study, the theological controversy in the speculative order should in no way hamper the work of effectively filling the ranks of the religious state with suitable members, if *the practice* as outlined and provided for in ecclesiastical legislation is followed.

ARTICLE 2. FURTHER SPECIFICATIONS OF CANON 538

a. The elements of Catholicity and freedom from impediments

That only baptized Catholics are able to become members of the canonical state of perfection almost goes without saying. Non-baptized persons, including catechumens, by the very nature of things do not enjoy the rights and privileges of members of the Church, (25) and baptized non-Catholics are excluded from those same rights and privileges since, even though in good faith, they juridically are held as excommunicated until reconciled with the Church and received into

---

give him understanding and good sense. Cf. also Simon, *Guidance of Religious* [an English translation of Watterott, *Ordensleitung*] (St. Louis: B. Herder, 1950), p. 364. According to the latter author, "if candidates bring along healthy natural dispositions, the work of their religious and ascetic training is easy."—p. 370; cf. the entire chapter, "Candidates for Religious Life," pp. 362-372.

(25) Cf. can. 87.

it. (26) While they might practice the evangelical counsels even by vow, therefore, and profitably, indeed, as regards their eternal salvation, they cannot be said to be doing so properly (*recte*) outside the fold of the Church, and in no way are they appropriately designated as "Religious." (27) In a word, non-Catholicity is an absolutely invalidating impediment to the juridic religious state. This hindrance can become rectified only upon reception into the Church. (28)

Other impediments (in addition to the already mentioned prohibitions contained in the natural law (29) and in particular constitutions) (30) which today debar entrance into the religious state are the following:

Admission is invalid in the case of:

Persons who have adhered to a non-Catholic sect; (31)
Persons who have not attained the required age; (32)

(26) Cf. can. 1325, §2, for the definition of apostasy, heresy and schism, and can. 2314, §1, regarding the penalties for them. While formal heresy only is punished in canon 2314, nevertheless in the external forum non-Catholics are not free from the effects of the canon, for in accordance with canon 2200, when there is the external violation of a law of the Church, malice is presumed in the external forum until its absence has been proved. Wherefore the Holy See insists that all converts from heretical or schismatical sects shall not be received into the Church until they have abjured their heresy or schism and been absolved from the censure. Cf. the Instruction of the Holy Office, July 20, 1859—*Fontes*, n. 953; *Concillii Plenarii Baltimorensis II, in Ecclesia Metropolitana Baltimorensi, a die VII ad diem XXI Octobris, A.D., MDCCCLXVI, Habiti et a Sede Apostolica Recogniti, Acta et Decreta* (ed. 2., Baltimore: Murphy, 1894) n. 242; cf. also Goodwine, *The Reception of Converts*, The Catholic University of America Canon Law Studies, n. 198 (Washington, D. C.: Catholic University of America Press, 1944), pp. 2-15, 100-102, 117-163.

(27) Cf. Urrutia, "Familiae Religiosae apud Anglicanos," *CpRM*, XXVII (1948), 90-103. On the other hand, Oriental Catholics who embrace the evangelical counsels in accord with the Oriental discipline are true religious, even though they do not follow the common life. Cf. Logar "Conspectus Historico Juridicus Juris Religiosorum Orientalium," *CpRM*, XXVI (1947), 271; *supra*, p. 15.

(28) Converts to the faith are not forbidden to become religious. The Commission for the Authentic Interpretation of the Code was asked whether the invalidating impediment of canon 542, *qui sectae acatholicae adhaeserunt*, applied to those who, moved by the grace of God, came into the Church from the heresy or schism in which they were born, or rather to those who fell away from the faith and joined a non-Catholic sect. The reply was: in the negative to the first part; in the affirmative to the second (16 oct. 1919, n. 7—*AAS*, XI [1919], 477). In a later response the Commission declared that persons who belong or have belonged to an atheistic sect are to be considered, as regards all legal effects, the same as persons who belong or have belonged to a non-Catholic sect (30 iul. 1934—*AAS*, XXVI (1934), 494.

(29) Cf. *supra*, p. 94.

(30) Cf. *supra*, p. 95, note (12).

(31) Cf. *supra*, note (28).

(32) One must be at least fifteen years of age for valid entrance into the novitiate (can. 555), sixteen years of age for temporary profession, and twenty one years of age for perpetual profession (can. 573).

Persons compelled to enter the religious state through grave fear, through deceit, or through force, or who are admitted by a superior thu constrained;

Married persons for the duration of the marriage;

Persons who are or have been professed members of another religious institute;

Persons subject to penalty for grave crimes of which they have been or may be accused;

Either residential or titular bishops, even though they have only been designated by the Roman Pontiff, and have not yet been consecrated;

Clerics who by a disposition of the Holy See are bound through an oath to devote themselves to the service of their diocese or of the missions, for that period of time for which their oath binds them. (33)

Admission is illicit, but valid, in the case of:

Clerics in major orders whose admission has not been made a matter of consultation with their Bishop, or to which he is opposed because their leaving the diocese would result in grave detriment to souls, which cannot otherwise be averted;

Those who have debts to pay and cannot settle the obligations;

Persons who are under the obligation of giving an account (e.g., for positions of trust), or who are implicated in other secular affairs, which might involve the religious organization in lawsuits and other annoyances;

Children whose parents, that is, father, mother, grandfather, grandmother, are in great want and in need of help, and parents whose work is needed for the maintenance and education of their children;

Candidates for the priesthood in a religious community if they suffer from an irregularity or any other canonical impediment;

Catholics of an Oriental Rite into religious organizations of the Latin Rite without the written permission from the Sacred Congregation for the Oriental Church; (34)

Those who have left a seminary. (35)

Even a cursory reading of these impediments makes it evident that neither are they very severe nor do they affect the great majority of Catholic youth. Certainly they are clearly enough stated, so that they are at least vaguely discernible in a particular case, in which contingency prudence would dictate a closer examination of the situation in the light of authoritative pronouncements of the Holy See and the commentaries of recognized canonists, as found in works readily available. (36) It is not within the scope of this study to examine them in detail.

---

(33) Can. 542, 1°. Ignorance of these impediments does not excuse from the law. Cf. can. 16.

(34) Can. 542, 2°.

(35) This last named impediment derives from a decree issued jointly by the Sacred Congregation of Religious and the Sacred Congregation of Seminaries and Universities on July 25, 1941—*AAS*, XXXI (1941), 371; cf. also *The Jurist*, II (1942), 380-382. The term *has left* is to be taken strictly; hence superiors may receive a seminarian who leaves a seminary in order to enter a religious institute. Cf. the reply of the Sacred Congregation of Religious, May 11, 1942—Bouscaren, *Digest*, II, 166.

(36) Cf., for example, Schaefer, *De Religiosis*, pp. 423-449; Wernz-Vidal, *De Religiosis*, pp. 195-214; Creusen-Garesché-Ellis, *Religious Men and Women*, pp. 133-138; Coronata, *Institutiones*, I, 708-716; Cappello, *Summa Iuris Canonici* (3 vols., Vol. I and II, 4. ed., 1945, Vol. III, 3. ed., 1948, Romae: Apud Aedes Universitatis Gregoriannae), II, 45-49; Brown,

A word might pertinently be said here, however, of a not too uncommon problem confronting well-intentioned and dutiful youths who, desiring to enter the religious state, are puzzled in certain cases as to the extent of their obligations towards their parents. Now the law clearly forbids the religious life to children whose parents are in great physical want and in need of their help, and obviously a youth who is the sole support of his aged mother or ailing father, or both, would have an obligation to them that would exclude, for the time being at least, any thought of entering the religious life. It is not in such cases of physical need, therefore, that a question is raised, for here the child's obligations are evident, and a dictate of the natural law itself. The problem arises rather in the face of what might be designated a "moral need" of an aspirant's parents, under which term the writer wishes to include spiritual, mental and emotional states. For it may happen that a child's (particularly an only child's) leaving for the religious life will have a disturbing effect on his parents within these areas, and as a result he might conclude that, in view of the circumstances, his vocation seems to be rather to assist his parents in their deficiency than to become a religious. The situation has arisen often enough not to be belabored with description here.

Now the problem admittedly is a delicate one. There are situations, certainly, in which this moral necessity is grave and arises out of human weakness and frailty rather than out of mere malice or bad will, and although the law is silent on the matter, by analogy with the prescription on physical want, it seems that, in such circumstances, a candidate should be persuaded to at least defer his entrance into the religious state. (37) It is a matter for prudent judgment, however, and much will depend on a careful weighing of the relative good and evil which such an act will occasion.

On the other hand, as has been too often the case, parental opposition can arise out of pure selfishness, (38) and as such need not deter an otherwise quali-

---

Religious Impediments; Koesler, *Entrance into the Novitiate by Clerics in Major Orders*, The Catholic University of America Canon Law Studies, n. 327 (Washington, D. C. Catholic University of America Press, 1952)

(37) Cf. Coronata, *Institutiones*, I, 715; Beste, *Introductio*, p. 367; Schaefer, *De Religiosis*, p. 443; Wernz-Vidal, *De Religiosis*, p. 211. The last named authors think that the circumstance is comprehended in the law itself.

(38) Parents should carefully ponder the words of Pope Pius XI in his memorable encyclical *Ad catholici sacerdotii fastigium*, 20 dec. 1935: "Yet it must be confessed with sadness that only too often parents seem to be unable to resign themselves to the priestly or religious vocations of their children. Such parents have no scruple in opposing the divine call with objections of all kinds; they even have recourse to means which can imperil not only the vocation of a more perfect state, but also the very conscience and the eternal salvation of those souls they ought to hold so dear. This happens all too often in the case even of parents who glory in being sincerely Christian and Catholic, especially in the higher and more cultured classes. This is a deplorable abuse. . . . The lack of vocations in families of the middle and upper classes may be partly explained by the dissipations of modern life, the seductions,

fied candidate from embracing the religious life. (39) A child has no obligations in the matter towards his parents who are so disposed. But here, too, caution must be exercised on the part of vocational directors. To advise a son or daughter to act directly against the wishes of his or her parents is a serious matter in any case, and particularly should the effects of alienation upon the candidate himself be taken into account. Some individuals are bound by much closer family ties than others, and the exercise of heroic virtue is not to be expected of all. It could be the better part of prudence at times, therefore, not to insist too strongly that one disregard one's parents' opposition, even though they be patently in the wrong. It is the good of the individual himself which prompts this decision, for it might be seen that estrangement from one's family will occasion for a person more harm than would be counteracted by the good to be achieved by him in the religious state. (40)

b. The element of right intention

The presence of a right intention in a candidate has been seen to be the element of signal importance in the matter of religious vocation; it is the all-necessary theological and juridical basis not only of the internal divine call, but also of the external ecclesiastical summons, to the religious state. No matter what theological system one chooses in order to account for its presence, a right intention is the result of man's effective cooperation with God's grace; of its

---

which especially in the larger cities, prematurely awaken the passions of youth; the schools in many places which scarcely conduce to the development of vocation. Nevertheless, it must be admitted that such a scarcity reveals a deplorable falling off of faith in the families themselves. . . . A long and sad experience has shown that a vocation betrayed—the word is not to be thought too strong—is a source of tears not only for the sons but also for the ill-advised parents; and God grant that such tears be not so long delayed as to become eternal tears."—*AAS*, XXVIII (1936), 48 (translation by Carroll, *Vocations Concern All Catholics* (Notre Dame, Indiana: Ave Maria Press, 1949), pp. 20-22.

(39) Cf. Coronata, *loc. cit.;* Beste, *loc. cit.*

(40) It should properly be noted that a minor (i.e., one who has not yet attained his twenty-first year of age) in the exercise of his rights remains subject to the power of his parents or guardians, except as regards those matters in which the law frees minors from parental control (cans. 88, 89.) Canons 542 and 555, §1, since they make no mention of parental consent when declaring the conditions for entrance into the religious life, implicitly exempt minors from parental control in the matter of their vocation once they have become fifteen years of age. According to the civil law, some states emancipate children from parental authority at the age of eighteen, and even in those states in which children reach their majority at twenty-one years there is little danger of a child's being forced to return to the home of his parents, if he can prove that he left it of his own accord. Cf. Jone-Adelman, *Moral Theology* (Westminster, Md.: Newman, 1945), p. 177; Creusen-Garesché-Ellis, *Religious Men and Women, in the Code* p. 138. In order to avoid possible civil litigation, however, superiors should familiarize themselves with the civil law on emancipation, and in the event of unjustified opposition on the part of parents they will have to determine in each individual case what account is to be taken of such opposition.

very nature it is something supernatural, and without it a vocation simply does not exist. This salient fact has been sufficiently demonstrated above. (41)

What is of interest here is the specific form this intention must take before it can be correctly designated as "right", a question which at first glance does not seem to present too much difficulty. Obviously it must include the efficacious will to achieve the ends of the religious life by using the means necessary for that attainment. Broken down into its component parts, as developed in the preceding pages, this simply means that the prospective candidate must aspire to perfection and intend to attain it by faithfully keeping the vows of poverty, chastity and obedience, and by living according to the rules and constitutions proper to his particular community, thereby incidentally contributing to the secondary aims of that institute. (42) Farrell, it has been seen, in his penetrating theological analysis has demonstrated with great clarity that this "*propositum religionis*" has as its principle, or is an elicited act of, the virtue of religion, specifically and actually an act of devotion in a most intense degree and magnanimous mode. The religious candidate with a true vocation, in other words, aspires to greatness in the sight of God; he wants to do great things for Christ. (43)

Less technically, a right intention is one which, in some way at least, is supernatural: to love God more, to seek the spiritual welfare of one's soul, to atone for one's sins, to better insure eternal salvation, etc., all are proper and commendable motives for entering the religious state and congruous with its pri-

---

(41) Cf. *supra*, pp. 34-36; 46-47; 48-51; 53-63; 64; 68; 72; 73-75; 76; 77, note (45); 81-82; 84; 86.

(42) The purpose to persevere in the religious life is a necessary component of the right intention, whether perpetual or only temporary vows are taken according to the particular constitutions of the respective institutes making up the religious state. This is sufficiently indicated in canon 488, 1°, which states that temporary vows are to be renewed when the time of the vows expires, and canon 577, §1, which directs that when the term of temporary vows expires there be no delay in renewal. Otherwise the stability required for the religious state by canon 487 would be absent. Wherefore Wernz-Vidal say that no one would be a true religious if he took temporary vows without the intention of renewing them at their expiration, "although in the external forum he would be held as such, since the internal intention contrary to the religious state would not be known." Cf. *De Religiosis*, p. 13. This is not contrary to canon 637, which speaks of the right of the person who has made temporary vows to freely leave the community at the expiration of the term for which such vows were taken, for this liberty is founded in a cause which arises *after* the taking of the vows, and not in a reservation made at the time of profession. Cf. Wernz-Vidal, *op. cit.*, p. 9 note (11).

(43) The study and exposition of the virtues of religion and magnanimity and their role in religious vocation, as well as of the various other factors and elements influencing religious vocation by positively promoting, or at least by establishing, the conditions necessary for the exercise of these two virtues are the proper province of the theologian. Father Farrell's *Theology of Religious Vocation* is most highly recommended by the present writer as being the outstanding work in this field.

mary end. Concomitant with this primary intention, but subordinated to it, are the secondary motives which can influence one to embrace the religious state: to care for the sick, for example, to labor among the poor, to teach in schools, to do catechetical work, to care for wayward youth, etc., far from being unworthy incentives, are laudibly directed to the secondary ends of the religious life. (44) As long as excessive and inordinate pre-occupation with these employments does not interfere with the attainment of the primary purpose of the religious state, that of personal perfection, (45) they can be of real spiritual value to the religious, for not least among the means to perfection, certainly, is that activity of love which finds expression in working directly for one's neighbor, and especially for the needs of one's neighbor. Because these ends are good in themselves, so is it good, therefore, to be motivated by them. First things must come first, however, and since the principal end of the religious state is self-perfection, the desire for self-perfection must be the principal motive influencing a religious candidate. (46)

But, on the other hand, anyone having even a superficial acquaintance with plain facts, and some reading knowledge of scientific psychopathology, knows that vocations may be followed through from wrong motives. True, this phenomenon is of relatively rare occurrence, but the fact of its rarity should not blind anyone to the possibility of its happening. Obviously, to seek admission

---

(44) Cf. Beste, *Introductio*, p. 361; Blat, *Commentarium*, II, Pars II et III, p. 270; Berutti, *Institutiones*, III, 131; Schaefer, *De Religiosis*, p. 409; *supra*, pp. 46-47, 50, 84, and the authorities there cited.

(45) This has very particular application to the period of the novitiate, for while the Code does not forbid *all* secondary activities during that time, studies or other occupation must not be so extensive as to interfere with the special religious formation, which is the main purpose of the novitiate. Cf. can. 565, §3: "Anno novitiatus ne destinentur novitii concionibus habendis aut audiendis confessionibus aut exterioribus religionis muniis, neve dedita opera studiis vacent litterarum, scientiarum aut artium; conversi autem in ipsa religiosa domo eatenus tantum fungi possunt officiis fratrum conversorum (non tamen uti primarii officiales), quatenus ab exercitiis novitiatus pro ipsis constitutis non praepediantur." The Sacred Congregation of Religious, on November 3, 1921, issued an Instruction for the second year of the novitiate also, the principal points of which are the following: 1) the spiritual formation of the novices shall be considered before every other duty; 2) the novices may be employed in the works of the institute if this is prescribed by the constitutions and, if their training demand it, the novices may be sent to other houses of the institute to be employed in the works of the institute, but only in a secondary capacity and under the direction and supervision of an older religious. The fact that there are not sufficient religious in some houses to carry on the works of the institute is never to be considered as a sufficient cause for sending novices out of the novitiate; 3) two months before the time for profession the novice must put aside all exterior works so as to have leisure to prepare for this great act in the novitiate house itself.—*AAS*, XIII (1921), 539.

(46) Cf. Blat, *loc. cit.*: "Nec putamus rectam intentionem, quae oculum haberet principaliter directam ad finem proprium alicuius religionis, principali et omnibus religionibus communi omnino praetermisso."

to the religious life for the purpose of obtaining honor or dignities, to make an "impression" on relatives and friends, or to be well provided for, etc., are motives which are natural in the sense of reflecting a wrong intention as opposed to a "right intention." (47) So patently foreign to the spirit of sacrifice and self-immolation which make up the very essence of the religious state, these and their like are by no means valid reasons for entering that state, and the point needs no elaboration.

Not so obviously seen as inadequate, however, particularly by the candidates themselves, are some "religious vocations" which actually are nothing but a disguise for a real problem which these individuals are unwilling to face in the reality of life, perhaps being the result of an effort to garb in a religious habit some deficiency or disappointment. In such instances the religious life becomes a poor second choice, a transient need, or "an out" to a difficulty. Granted that motives may be simple or complex, also sometimes quite vague in the aspirant's mind, and not to forget that external graces often take diverse forms; it still remains that the right intention demanded by canon 538 in its correlation to canons 488, 1°, and 593 must in some way be supernatural, and where a motive gives little hope of growing to that supernatural character, a candidate cannot be accepted as having a right intention. As has been stated in the preceding article, much can be accomplished with basically good material through a proper education and by means of a genuine direction of values, a fact recognized in canon 565, §1, and not to be overlooked by religious superiors; but it is also a fact of experience that not all such attempts at correction are successful, and a superior is bound by the law to admit failure in this regard rather than, by receiving an obviously unsuited candidate, to have a hand in his possible eternal failure and the harm which such a one can bring to the religious state. (48)

c. *The element of suitability* (idoneitas)

It may once again be noted that, in general, the qualities demanded in candidates for the religious life are neither too exacting nor are they such as not to be possessed by the majority of Catholic youth, a truth which is as readily admitted by the proponents of the special vocation theory as by those who hold to the general vocation concept. Which is as it should be, for as Farrell states:

---

(47) Cf. Beste, *loc. cit.;* Blat, *loc. cit.;* Berutti, *loc. cit.;* Schaefer, *loc. cit.; supra*, pp. 47, note (62); 77, note (45); 80.

(48) It is merely recalled here that, although an intention is essentially something internal, it also is a matter for the external forum, for it manifests itself there in words, actions, attitudes, etc. It is these external indications upon which a superior bases his judgment. Cf. *supra*, pp. 58-59. Cf. also Parente, *Spiritual Direction* (St. Meinrad, Indiana: Abbey Press, 1950), p. 70: "Intention manifests itself, often unconsciously, in many different ways. The interests, the likes and dislikes, the enthusiasms, hobbies of a person are an index of the secret tendency of the soul, especially when they are more less constant and uniform."

The fact (must be taken into account) that all men are by divine invitation called upon to consider the religious life as a state suitable to themselves. Hence, the natural qualities making an individual fitted for the religious state must be flexible enough to bring within their limits at least the majority of normal persons, otherwise mother nature leaves herself open to the charge of niggardliness in things useful, or even necessary for life. (49)

But it is just as true, and important enough to be repeated once more, hat certain fundamental needs and basic qualifications in aspirants to the religious life cannot be dispensed with. In the words of Saint Augustine

Many have sincerely promised that they would live up to that holy calling, which holds all things in common, where no one calls anything his own, which has but one heart and soul in God; but when they were placed in the furnace, they cracked. (50)

"The cracking" may not only be disastrous for the individual, but, as has been pointed out, can adversely affect the religious state itself.

The Code of Canon Law does not go into specific detail on its requirement "*ad religionis onera ferenda idoneus*," an understandable omission in view of the diversity to be found among the various institutes and their characteristic modes of activity in the religious life, but leaves the matter for the most part to the discretion of superiors. Nevertheless, legal inference from the Code's description of the essential nature of the religious life gives a common denominator applicable to all forms of that life, and in general demands physical, mental and moral equipment which offers a well-founded hope that the candidate will not be found defective in carrying out the duties of his chosen state. Whether the latter takes the form of a life of work in behalf of others or merely that of a special regime of prayer and sacrifice, the religious life demands a normally strong constitution and well-balanced mind and nervous system. Considerable deformity or great bodily debility, although not disgraceful to the individual, can present an insuperable obstacle to leading a full religious life, and in addition may draw ridicule, however unjustly, upon a religious community and the religious state in general. Likewise, sufficient mental aptitude to grasp the essential notions of the religious life is indispensable. While brilliance or exceptional ability is not required, the ability to learn cannot be of too low a degree even in the case of those whose duties revolve about manual labor and the service of others, because to be a good religious, even as a lay brother, it is necessary to be able to understand many things pertaining to prayer, obedience, fidelity to rule, the interior life, etc. (51)

---

(49) *The Theology of Religious Vocation*, p. 143.

(50) *The Monastic Life*, quoted in *The Christian Life*, compiled from the works of Saint Augustine by Tonna-Barthet (New York: Pustet, 1929), p. 601.

(51) This is particularly the implication of canon 565, §1. Cf. also §2 of the same canon: "The candidates for lay brothers (or lay sisters) must, moreover, be thoroughly instructed in Christian doctrine, for which purpose a special instruction shall be given to them at least once a week."

As to the moral requirements, the guiding norm may be proposed as "ordinary piety and sound habits of virtue." For while sanctity is the goal of, and not a requirement for, the religious state, and progress in virtue its *raison d'etre*, candidates even for the novitiate, which has for its purpose the "eradication of faulty habits, the control of the passions and the acquisition of virtues," (52) must give evidence of such dispositions of soul as to offer a well-founded hope that they will persevere in their good resolve and meet the minimum requirements of moral fitness demanded by the Church of religious from the very beginning. This is not to deny to a person the possibility completely to conquer the habits of vice or any great propensities to sin, and indeed such a one has great need of spiritual direction, but with the religious state existing as a form of life in common and a public ecclesiastical state, the Church has obligations towards other members of the community and the faithful at large, which do not allow it to endanger their spiritual welfare in the process of training one individual. His "religious formation" must take place privately and not in the public state of perfection. (53)

This has particular and evident application with regard to the virtues of obedience and moral purity. As to the former, it has already been pointed out (54) that an "individualist" can easily disturb the internal peace and good order necessary for the spiritual advancement of the group and the effective carrying out of its work. Cooperation and docility are indispensable requisites to be sought in every member of the religious state, and while one should grow in the spirit of humility and obedience as he advances on the road to perfection, one never should be so lacking in these virtues as to seriously upset the harmony of the community. Granted that a person of good will may under direction overcome his grave deficiency in time, the principle of the common good demands that he receive that direction outside of the religious state.

Similarly the moral purity of a religious is not only a personal concern, but the concern of the entire body of religious and the Church itself. No other characteristic of the religious life has greater prominence in or brings greater honor and esteem to that state than the observance of this angelic virtue by its members, and conversely no other vice plays so destructive a role in the religious life as that of impurity. Therefore, what has been said above concerning the vow of perpetual continence taken outside the canonical state of perfection, viz., the prudence and care which must be exercised before such a consequential step is

---

(52) Can. 565, §1.

(53) In the light of this consideration must be viewed Farrell's statement: "This condition (powerful inclinations to sin and recent or still enduring habits of vice) must not be considered a deterrent from entrance into religion; rather it is a state of the subject which will make somewhat difficult the deliberation necessary ordinarily for a religious vocation."—*op. cit.*, p. 159 note (69).

(54) Cf. *supra*, pp. 68-69.

taken lest one endanger his eternal salvation by assuming more than he can bear, (55) has additional emphasis when applied to the life of continence in the religious state. For in the latter instance grave deordination harms not only the individual but, as is evident, can have a dire effect on the entire religious state. The good of the Church can regularly be served only by chaste religious, and a doubt concerning a candidate's fitness in this matter must not be resolved in favor of the individual. Again, the common good demands otherwise. (56)

As a general description of a suitable subject for the religious life, therefore, the words of Farrell may be adopted:

> Presupposed to what may be called the ordinary or usual religious vocation, is a subject of normal health and with sufficient strength to perform the work of a religious; with the mental capacity to grasp the essential meaning of the religious life as a great way of serving God and to digest fairly well, at least to the extent of being able to put into practice, the direction and counsel received from those in a position to give it; free from those powerful inclinations to sins and the impediments to devotion and magnanimity which result from recent or still enduring habits of sin; and finally in the state of grace when the divine vocation is constituted, with a will informed by the virtues of religion and magnanimity from which vocation to the religious life flows. (57)

In the concrete, of course, as has been explained above, these general principles of fitness are adapted and applied according to the particular nature and special requirements of each particular institute. An institute which engages in foreign mission work, to give an obvious example, will require higher standards of physical fitness than one which has the care of orphans at home as its special work. Again, one should not overlook temperamental directives and the possession of special talents as aids in determining where one might best serve God, the Church and himself in the religious life. As to the former, it is true that temperaments do not exist in persons as so many pure types; people rather possess characteristics of several types, and this in varying degrees. But the

---

(55) Cf. *supra*, pp. 65-66.

(56) A detailed study of the virtue of chastity and its application to the religious state is properly the province of moral theologians and therefore will not be engaged in here. Moreover, except in obvious cases wherein the subject has great proclivity to sensuality and is the victim of bad habits, it is difficult to give a general norm; each case presents a separate study, and all attending circumstances must be taken into account. The observation of Biot and Galimard is pertinent: "Pour juger de la valeur d'un jeune homme ou d'une jeune fille, une étude attentive de sa famille entière s'impose. Il n'entre pas seul au seminaire, elle ne franchira pas seule la clôture. Du fait qu'ila pénètrent avec tout leur passé psychologique, c'est un peu leur famille aussi qui y entre avec eux, car leur passé, c'est elle."—*Guide Medical des Vocations Sacerdotales et Religieuses* (Paris, 1945), p. 132. Cf. also *ibidem*, p. 172: "Il faut considérer qu'à 20 ou 21 ans l'orientation de la sexualité doit être stable et definitive et que par consequent toute déviation de la libido constitue une contreindication absolue." Vromant has this to say about the matter: "Peccatum mortale pollutionis solitariae, durante novitiatu, semel vel bis deliberate admissum, dimissionem enixe suadet." "De signis negativis vocationis sacerdotalis et religiosae" (*Periodica*, XXII [1933], 191.)

(57) *The Theology of Religious Vocation*, p. 159.

writer holds with those who think that rough classifications of people according to predominant temperaments can be made, and that these are very useful for self-knowledge and for finding the particular occupations for which one is best suited. (58)

But, whereas temperament indicates a direction, talents are more specific. The religious state has need for men of ability in almost every field, and it is usually true that one would do better to join a religious institute in which his particular abilities and gifts can best be utilized for the benefit of that society's special work. This is not an absolute rule, however, for among ordinary people there is a certain transfer of abilities. A good mathematician, in other words, need not join a teaching order, nor a nurse a nursing order; they may well derive greater spiritual benefit from becoming members of an institute which engages in a totally unrelated type of specialized activity. It is the personal perfectioning of oneself, it must be remembered, that is *the* primary reason for the religious state's existence. In general, however, the great variety of institutes which make up the juridic religious state is a sure guarantee that no fit subject will be at a loss in finding one which is well suited to his or her needs, dispositions, interest and talents.

---

(58) A good, if rather technical, description of the temperaments may be found in Tanquerey-Branderis, *The Spiritual Life*, pp. 8*-14*.

Chapter VII
SUMMARY

The body of this study having now been concluded, the writer wishes to state by way of introduction to a brief summary that he is intellectually convinced of the validity of the Thomistic position on the controversial subjects of divine grace, predestination and free will. By force of the weight of objective arguments advanced by the proponents of this system, and with no attempt being made here either to substantiate his opinion or to criticize opposing theories, he holds that efficacious grace *entitatively* and *intrinsically* differs from sufficient grace; that an efficacious "will" act is the result of a grace, *particular* both in an extensive and qualitative sense, which moves the will *freely* but *infallibly* to the attainment of its object; that *it is not* the consequence of essentially the same graces given to all men which happen to be *rendered efficacious* in a particular instance by the consent of man.

From the mere statement of this persuasion, therefore, it logically and necessarily follows that the writer either espouses the special divine vocation theory or else is guilty of the same inconsistency which he has attributed to others. The first observation is correct: the writer firmly believes that God has eternally predestined certain individuals in preference to others for the religious state no less than for the priesthood, in time endowing them with the qualities needed for valid and lawful acceptance into that state *and* with the special and particular grace required to make the efficacious "*propositum religionis assumendae;*" he holds that the efficacious grace of a religious vocation is the result of a divine decree *antecedent* to man's use of free will, and *not consequent* or dependent upon man's choice, and that without this special grace of vocation which is not given to all, a religious vocation is non-existent.

And yet it is most emphatically stated that this concept of divine religious vocation as here presented has *not* been gained as a conclusion of the study just completed. It is the logical consequence of a legitimately held *theological theory* on grace, based on what are believed to be solid premises, but it is not the juridic concept of religious vocation which, while recognizing what is theologically certain in the question of religious vocation, viz., the necessity of a divine call given through supernatural grace, does not exclusively adopt any particular system to explain the specific nature of that grace. The problem of how the providence of God and His efficacious grace is to be reconciled with man's free will is deeply mysterious, because there are too many elements in it which do not yield to our gaze. By adopting one of the theological systems one feels towards a reconciliation, or perhaps better gropes in the direction where the reconciliation may prove to be, but that is all. The present law of the Church, on the other hand, since it permits any of the several acceptable theories on grace to be held, and in its prescripts on admission into the religious state does not favor any particular system, is seen as the legislator's practical norm of action in the face of a speculative controversy, and in its expression is eminently acceptable both to those who profess the general divine vocation theory, as well as to those who espouse the special vocation concept.

Actually, as stated above, the writer by invoking the Thomistic doctrine to explain the nature and activity of the efficacious vocational grace espouses the latter, and interprets canon 538 accordingly, but this is made known here, upon consideration, merely for the purpose of emphasizing and underlining the fact that the conclusions of this study would in no way be affected if the Suarezian system on grace and the general vocation theory were held. The law of the Church demands positive evidence of the presence of a divine vocation (manifested particularly by a right intention), but leaves the speculative problem of its specific nature in the speculative domain, to be examined and answered by the theologians. Perhaps the right intention required by the law *is* the result of a special grace which is given only to the subjects of God's predilection; then again, perhaps it is the result of a grace given to all men, but specified and rendered efficacious in a particular instance by the consent of man: the *law* does not say: it merely requires the presence of a right intention, no matter how formed.

This view, it has been seen, is not in accord with that of most of the authors. Some have been criticized for saying that canon 538 excludes the notion of a special divine vocation because it does not mention it; others have been accused of reading too much into the canon when they say it is either the equivalent of or a necessary presupposition for a special divine call. Coronata's statement that the Code seems unwilling to solve the question, and is indifferent whether the canonically qualified candidate has received a special or a general vocation, is perhaps the closest approach to the conclusion of this study, although he subsequently qualifies his observation by citing the comparative phrasing of canons 538 and 1353 to substantiate his preference for the general divine vocation concept.

A recently published work on religious vocation, a doctoral dissertation submitted to the Faculty of the Pontifical University of the Lateran for the degree of Doctor of Both Laws, (1) deserves a word of special comment, which will incidentally further illustrate the conclusion of this study. The author, Father Ladislaus of the Congregation of the Passion, definitely holds that the general

(1) P. Ladislaus a Maria Immaculata, *De Vocatione Religiosa* (Romae: Apud Studiorum Domum C.P., 1950.) Inasmuch as this work was not available to the writer until this study had been completed and submitted for approval, it has not been previously cited. The author utilizes many of the same canonical texts to be found in the present study and therefore is an outstanding exception to the observation made on page 53, note (88), *supra*.

divine vocation theory lacks any semblance of a solid foundation, that "there exists for the religious state a divine vocation which is and must be called special, not only because it is specified in individuals, but *also in so far as it is not given to all.*" (2) To substantiate this thesis he presents arguments based on Scripture, the writings of the Fathers, certain doctors and theologians of the Church, and what is of pertinent interest here, the Code of Canon Law and juridical documents. (3)

Now, the present writer wishes to make two things clear: firstly, he is in absolute agreement with the *conclusion* expressed by Father Ladislaus that a religious vocation is the result of a *special* call from Almighty God, but he *is* in agreement principally because of *theological* convictions not expressed in that author's work, nor demonstrated in his own; secondly, while certain canonical texts contained in this study, and also cited by Father Ladislaus, have been pointed out by the present writer as seeming "better understood in the light of the special divine vocation theory . . . some indeed which on the surface appear definitely misleading apart from it," (4) it has also been very definitely pointed out by the writer that these texts, indicative as they are, have not been the whole story of the legislator's mind on the specific nature of the divine call to the religious state, and in illustration of this fact other texts have been cited, particularly with reference to the institute of the "*pueri oblati*," which not only seem in accord with the general vocation theory, but even opposed to the special vocation concept, (5) the resulting legislative pattern being termed as "apparently cloudy." (6)

It is interesting to note Father Ladislaus's view on the juridic concept of divine religious vocation. The canonical sources cited in his work, and referred to above, are first of all and principally used as an aid for establishing the legislator's historical recognition of the existence and necessity of the divine vocation to the religious state, (7) and this, the writer agrees, they most clearly do. (8) Father Ladislaus goes further, however, when on the strength of these documents he states that "the Church in no way holds that all men have been called to keep the evangelical counsels in the religious state, but holds that only some have been called, who alone are able to be admitted into the

(2) *Op. cit.*, p. 121 (italics are the author's.)

(3) Cf. *ibidem*, especially pages 112-121, but also pages 8-111 *passim*, which contain the basic material for the argument presented. Canonical matter may be found on pages 28-31, 33-38, 56-59, 61-67, 84-93, 97-111, 116-117, 120-121.

(4) *Supra*, p. 48. These texts are to be found in the present study on pages 48-51, 63, note (124), and in Father Ladislaus's work on pages 29-31, 33-38, 61-67, 85, 88-93, 97-100.

(5) Cf. *supra*, pp. 44-46, 47-48.

(6) Cf. *supra*, p. 52. The writer's commentary on the import of these and like texts will be found *supra*, particularly on pages 52-53, 61-63.

(7) Cf. especially pp. 84-85, 88-93, but also the citations in note (3), *supra*.

(8) Cf. *supra*, pp. 46-47, 49-51.

religious state." (9) The contention of this study, on the other hand, has been that many of these texts were not of universal extent, that many others may be variously interpreted, while still others may have been the direct or indirect expression of the theological convictions of *some* of the persons who at different times in history have enjoyed legislative power in the Church, but do not necessarily represent the opinions of *all* who have held such power. (10) This last, it has been seen, is an argument of particular force in view of the legislator's long recognition of the institute of the "*pueri oblati.*"

Father Ladislaus also recognizes the "problem" which this canonical institute of child oblation presents to the advocates of the special vocation theory, but he simply does not offer a satisfactory solution; in fact, he does not even get to the core of the question. The practice itself is accurately stated and its long-lived juridical existence admitted, (11) but to argue as he does that, if one resorts to the general vocation theory to explain the Church's practice, one likewise admits that men could be forced to observe the evangelical counsels, and, on the contrary, to say that "the institute of the oblates is satisfactorily explained and the practice of the Church escapes all taint of crime, if the explanation of its existence is sought in the customs, the filial piety, and especially in the greater power of parents in those days," (12) is not to the point. The truth of the matter is that the Church for a long time *did* bind the oblate to the perpetual observance of the evangelical counsels in the religious state, and this "*velit nolit,*" in the words of Father Ladislaus himself, (13) and the present study, attempting neither to defend or even to explain the practice, has merely pointed it out as a very strong indication of the *legislator's mind* at the time that all men were given the grace to make the meritorious "*propositum religionis*" if they but willed to. In no way, it is argued, could the legislator's action be justified if he believed otherwise, i.e., if he believed that the grace of vocation was given only to some men and not to others. (14) The purpose of this study has been simply the presentation of this as a most probable inference from the legislator's action, not to criticize it. The writer disagrees with the opinion, it is true, but he disagrees for theological reasons which are as yet uncertain, (15) and since this is not a theological work, no attempt is made here to substantiate his stand.

As for the Code of Canon Law and the question of divine religious vocation, in this study seen as the legislator's practical norm of action in the face of a

(9) *Op. cit.*, p. 120.

(10) Cf. *supra*, pp. 52-53.

(11) *Op. cit.*, pp. 25-27. Many authors, councils, and popes are cited in proof of its legal existence.

(12) *Ibidem*, pp. 116-117; cf. also pp. 27-28.

(13) *Ibidem*, p. 116; cf. also pp. 26-28.

(14) Cf. *supra*, p. 45.

(15) Cf. *supra*, p. 42, note (37).

speculative controversy, (16) Father Ladislaus correctly points out that the law's silence on the matter of religious vocation is not to be equated to the law's denial of the existence of the vocation, and that commentators who seek approbation of their general vocation theory in the Code do so in vain, (17) a contention also to be found in these pages. (18) But he immediately adds that "this divine vocation (recognized by the Code) is to be called special . . . (for) although the ecclesiastical legislator did not wish openly to solve the question pertaining to religious vocation, much can be found in the Code which absolutely demands a special vocation." (19) The legislator, in other words, did not successfully accomplish his desire to remain, as a legislator, completely neutral on the vocation controversy. To this contention the writer opposes the conclusion stated above, and classifies Father Ladislaus among those authors who read more into the mind of the legislator of the Code than he has actually expressed in the phrasing of his law.

As a final word on this matter of the *divine* call, then, it is once again stated that the writer agrees with Father Ladislaus's *conclusion* on the necessity of a special divine vocation to the religious state; he also thinks that this author has done much to establish his contention by his use of Scripture, the writings of the Apostolic Fathers and Doctors of the Church, and that he has given it added emphasis by the exposition of certain ecclesiastical documents. But the writer denies that this conclusion is the *juridic concept* of religious vocation as it exists today.

The writer is also at odds with Father Ladislaus's view of the juridic concept of religious vocation on another score, viz., on the existence and the necessity of the ecclesiastical call to the religious state. For while that author goes to some lengths to prove that the matter of religious vocation very definitely belongs to the external forum of the Church and has a juridic note, so that it truly can be called canonical or juridical, (20) he just as positively holds that the ad-

---

(16) Cf. *supra*, pp. 53-63.

(17) *Op. cit.*, p. 117; cf. also pp. 86-88.

(18) Cf. *supra*, pp. 58-59, 60.

(19) *Loc. cit.* The entire passage reads as follows: "Silentium hoc in casu negationi aequipari non potest. Nam, uti demonstravimus, Codex sufficienter vocationis divinae necessitatem innuit, imo et indirecte admittit, quae vocatio, nunc addimus, specialis dicenda est. Frustra, censemus, commentatores quidam adprobationem theoriae vocationis generalis in Codice quaerunt. Quamvis legislator ecclesiasticus, ad vocationem religiosam quod spectat, questionem aperte dirimere noluerit, plura in Codice inveniri possunt, quae vocationem specialem omnino exigunt." The "*plura in Codice*" is understood by the present writer to be the author's reference to the institute of the novitiate, the discipline regarding the testimonial letters, the conditions enumerated in canon 538, and the phrase "*qui indicia praebeant ecclesiasticae vocationis*" of canon 1353, which Father Ladislaus applies to religious vocation (!). Cf. *op. cit.*, pp. 82-88.

(20) Cf. *op. cit.*, pp. 100-105. He answers two objections: "1) Vocatio religiosa, quae nihil aliud est quam Dei inspiratio, cum res sit fori interni, a iure attingi non potest, ideoque

mission of a candidate into the religious state by a legitimate superior is in no way to be considered as a vocation or an integral part of a vocation. The office of the superior is merely to discern between a true and a false *divine* vocation (the only vocation truly so called) and his acceptance of the candidate is no more than a necessary condition for valid and licit entrance into the religious state. (21) In proof of his thesis he states that the concept of an ecclesiastical call "is not founded in tradition: the Church teaches that there is one vocation to the religious state, even in the external forum, and it is that vocation which is called divine or theological. No document is found which speaks of a two-fold vocation." (22)

The present study, on the contrary, establishing its conclusion as a necessary deduction from the nature of the religious life as it exists today, an official school of perfection pursued in common under the authorization and direction of the Church, and a part of its public service, holds that the acceptance of a candidate by a legitimate superior is something more than an authoritative pronouncement on the presence of a divine vocation, which indeed it is. It has been seen also as an official invitation, or call, or vocation, by which ecclesiastical authority summons to profession those individuals whom it judges qualified to represent it in the religious state. The Church's invitation to profession is accordingly presented as no less imperative for valid and lawful entrance into the religious state than the ecclesiastical call is for lawful ordination to the priesthood, and as no less a *real vocation.* A religious vocation, in other words, is the composite of two calls, divine and ecclesiastical; with the absence of either, it simply does not exist. (23)

---

vocatio religiosa iuridica appellari non valet. 2) Ecclesia in suis documentis de vocatione religiosa agit eamque exigit. At si vocationis nomine intelligitur divinus afflatus, cum de illius existentia in foro externo certitudo obtineri nequeat, vocatio in sensu iuridico dici non potest."

(21) "[Traditionalis doctrina] semper hoc unum docuit: Deum tantum vocare et *proprie* vocare et *perfecte* vocare ad religionem; superiores vero ius et officium *solummodo* habere discernendi veram a falsa vocatione seu authentice declarandi an vocatio revera existat necne, admissionem, ut diximus, *condicionem tantum* esse ad religionem ingrediendam necessariam." —*op. cit.*, p. 110.

"Haec dumtaxat est vocatio [afflatus divinus] quam disciplina ecclesiastica requirit in postulantibus, de qua iudicium ultimum et auctoritativum legitimis religionis Superioribus reservat, quorum est in religionem candidatos admittere. Cetera omnia, quae exiguntur ut re vera quis, iuxta Ecclesiae disciplinam, religionem ingredi valeat, nonnisi condiciones sunt. Quae condiciones sunt quidem necessariae, sed *neque vocationem constituunt* neque *partem integrantem vocationis.*"—*op. cit.*, p. 111 (italics are the author's.)

(22) *Op. cit.*, p. 108; cf. also pp. 110-111. Father Ladislaus is not alone in holding this opinion. Cf., e.g., Olivero's observation *supra*, p. 7, note (13).

(23) Cf. *supra*, pp. 68-91; cf. also pp. 18-33, which contain the basic material for the later deduction.

The present writer feels that Father Ladislaus has missed the complete significance of the superior's acceptance of a candidate because, in concentrating his efforts on a refutation of the exaggerations of those who assign a relatively unimportant place to divine grace in the matter, (24) he has failed to recognize the truth as well as the error contained in their theories, and therefore has not given sufficient consideration to the nature of the religious life as a public, reserved state of the Church and the consequences which logically follow from the fact. Farrell, on the other hand, while holding to the special divine vocation concept no less than does Father Ladislaus, and giving primacy to the internal, passive vocation, (25) does not fail to give due recognition to the ecclesiastical call. (26)

In conclusion, then, it is once again stated that this study has been an exposition of the legislator's guiding norm of action in the question of religious vocation. To those who ask, "Have I a vocation to the religious state?" or "Has he or she a vocation?" he offers a rule of judgment which may safely and confidently be followed. The admitting superior is to measure the suitability of a candidate according to the objective standard of law, general and particular, and if the aspirant is not found wanting in any respect, the superior may invite or call him to profession. With that call the candidate can rest assured that he has received a religious vocation, divine as well as ecclesiastical, for the latter may not be given until assurance is had of the former, manifested at least through the presence of a right intention. Whether the right intention is the effect of a special

(24) Cf. *op. cit.*, especially pages 108-111, where he examines the theories of Vermeersch and Lahitton. Cf. also *supra*, pp. 36, 40-41, 55.

(25) " . . . theological thought previous to any of the theories exposed in these pages indicates definitely that primacy must be given to an internal, passive vocation."—*The Theology of Religious Vocation*, p. 28. Cf. also *ibidem*, p. 16.

(26) "Canon Lahitton's positive argument that the religious state, because it is reserved by ecclesiastical law, requires an external call by legitimate superiors, which call constitutes vocation strictly taken, contains both truth and error. From a juridical point of view an external, authoritative call by a superior's admittance of a candidate to the novitiate or the religious profession definitely constitutes a religious vocation. This much of the Canon's argument is certainly true. But he fails to consider that the juridical point of view does not bring into focus the whole of the religious state."—*op. cit.*, p. 27. On this latter point cf. what was said *supra*, p. 2: "A study which would so concentrate on the juridic aspect of religious vocation as to overlook or minimize the positiveness of God's role and His grace in the matter would give rise to no less an erroneous conclusion, despite whatever actual value such a study may have in contributing to an understanding of one or the other facet of the question."

"Considered from the juridical point of view . . . this call by legitimate superiors may be interpreted in a twofold manner. 1) It may be considered a stamp of approval on the suitability of the candidate as indicated by his external acts and condition . . . 2) as a juridical act conferring a privilege upon the candidate to enter into, or to make profession in, a religious institute."—Farrell, *ibidem*, pp. 82-83.

or a general grace, the law does not say; it merely postulates the intention, no matter how it is effected.

This, it is said, is a practical norm of action, and while truth and reality are not measured in terms of utility, and the writer hopes he would be the last to say that it matters little to know how God works in man—as if one could love God more by knowing less about Him—it should be acceptable to the proponents of either the special or the general divine vocation theory, as well as to those who follow the only system they know: the love of God in their hearts.

CONCLUSIONS

1. The religious state as founded by Christ and the religious state as it exists today, a canonical state of perfection and apostolic service, are not substantially coextensive. To the essential nature of the former, a fixed mode of life with self-perfection as its end and the evangelical counsels as its means, ecclesiastical legislation has added the elements of the common life, the common rule, and secondary ends, and has established the resulting entity as one of the three principal states in the Church. As such the religious state is of ecclesiastical institution and its members officially represent the Church both in the life of perfection and in the various fields of education, charity, and other apostolic activities.

2. As related in Scripture, Christ issued an external invitation to all men to live the life of evangelical perfection, and as it has been commonly interpreted by the Fathers and the theologians of the Church, past and present, this invitation was a general, external vocation to all men to enter the religious state, either in its private or public form.

3. But by reason of its essential nature, the life of perfection, whether lived privately or in the canonical state, cannot be efficaciously embraced except through an additional divine invitation or vocation given in the realm of grace. This is a necessary theological conclusion clearly recognized in juridical documents past and present.

4. The question of the specific nature of this grace of vocation, however, whether it is a special and particular grace given only to the subjects of God's predilection, antecedent to and not consequent upon their use of free will, or whether it is essentially the same graces given to all men which happen to be rendered efficacious in a particular instance by the consent of man, is a controverted matter among canonists as well as among theologians. To a great extent one's answer to the problem will be determined by one's adherence to one or the other theological system on grace, predestination and free will. Supporting arguments for both the general and the special vocation theory may be found in Scripture, in the Fathers, and in juridical documents, the authors of the last seeming at one time to favor one theory of divine vocation, and at another time its opposite.

5. The present law of the Church regulating admission into the religious state is the legislator's practical answer in the face of the speculative problem. Canon 538 demands the presence of a divine vocation in a candidate, manifested particularly by a right intention, but does not specify whether this is the result of a special or of a general divine call. Neither theory can claim to furnish an exclusive basis for the juridic concept of divine religious vocation; the law does

not favor or exclude either. By reason of the judgment of the Commission of Cardinals in 1912, only the unwarranted exaggerations of the attraction theory are absolutely untenable.

6. With regard to the juridic religious state, the divine call has its complement in the Church's official invitation to profession in an approved institute, so that the two vocations thus coalesce to produce the adequate concept of a religious vocation. Without the latter, one does not have a religious vocation no matter how fit a subject for the religious state one might be; with the call of the superior, a candidate is to be juridically regarded as having a divine vocation also, no matter how it is thought to be effected, for the ecclesiastical call may not lawfully be given apart from the presence of the divine vocation as manifested at least through the presence of a right intention.

7. In determining the suitability or the vocation of a candidate for the religious state, admitting superiors are to be guided by the objective reality of law. Canon 538, read in conjunction with the meaning and implications of canons 487, 488, 1°, 542, 562, 565, §1, and 593, contains the Church's explicit summation of the essential conditions and sufficient signs of a religious vocation, divine and ecclesiastical, which may be reduced to four elements: Catholicity; a right intention (i.e., one which in some way is supernatural), freedom from impediments of the natural law, the general ecclesiastical law, and of the particular law of the institute one wishes to enter; physical, mental and moral qualifications required by the religious life in general and corresponding to the requirements of at least one of the approved institutes in particular.

8. Religious vocations laudably may be fostered. The training and direction in the novitiate can do much in preparing basically equipped candidates for a religious vocation, but it is particularly in the good Catholic home where vocations are planted, take root and grow. The school and the parish priest also have important roles to play in this regard.

BIBLIOGRAPHY

Sources

Acta Apostolicae Sedis, Commentarium Officiale, Romae, 1909—

Acta Sanctae Sedis, 41 vols., Romae, 1865-1908.

Bouscaren, T. Lincoln, *The Canon Law Digest, Officially Published Documents Affecting the Code of Canon Law*, 2 vols. and Supplement through 1948, Milwaukee: The Bruce Publishing Co., 1934-1949.

Bruns, H., *Canones Apostolorum et Conciliorum Saeculorum IV-VII*, 2 vols., Berolini, 1839.

Bullarum Diplomatum et Privilegiorum Sanctorum Romanorum Pontificum Taurinensis Editio, 25 vols., Augustae Taurinorum, 1857-1872.

Canones et Decreta Sacrosancti Oecumenici Concilii Tridentini, Editio Novissima ad Fidem Optimorum Exemplarium castigate Impressa (XIX reimpressio stereotypa), Taurini, 1913.

Codex Iuris Canonici Pii X Pontificis Maximi iussu digestus, Benedicti Papae XV auctoritate promulgatus, Romae: Typis Polyglottis Vaticanis, 1917.

Codex Regularium Monasticarum et Canonicarum, ed. Lucas Holstenius, 6 vols., Romae, 1759.

Codicis Iuris Canonici Fontes, cura Eñi Petri Gasparri editi, 9 vols., Romae (postea Civitate Vaticana): Typis Polyglottis Vaticanis, 1923-1939. (Vols. VII-IX. ed. cura et studio Eñi Iustiniani Serédi.)

Collectanea in Usum Secretariae Sacrae Congregationis Episcoporum et Regularium, ed. noviss., A. Bizzarri, Romae, 1885.

Collectanea Sacrae Congregationis de Religiosis, Enchiridion de Statibus Perfectionis, Vol. I, *Documenta Ecclesiae Sodalibus Instituendis*, Romae: Officium Libri Catholici, 1949.

Collectio Lacensis: Acta et Decreta Sacrorum Conciliorum Recentium, 7 vols., Friburgi-Brisgoviae: Herder, 1870-1892.

Concilii Plenarii Baltimorensis II, in Ecclesia Metropolitana Baltimorensi, a die VII ad diem XXI Octobris A.D., MDCCCLXVI, Habiti, et a Sede Apostolica Recogniti, Acta et Decreta, 2. ed., Baltimorae: John Murphy, 1894.

Corpus Iuris Civilis, 3 vols., Berolini, 1928-1929. *Institutiones*, quas recognivit P. Krueger, ed. stereotypa 15., 1928; *Digesta*, quas recognivit T. Mommsen et retractavit P. Krueger, ed. stereotypa 15., 1928; *Codex Iustinianus*, quem recognovit et retractavit P. Krueger, ed. stereotypa 10., 1929; *Novellae*, quas recognovit R. Schoell, et absolvit G. Kroll, ed. stereotypa 5., 1928.

Decretales D. Gregorii Papae IX, una cum glossis restitutae, 2 vols., Romae, 1582.

Decretum Gratiani emendatum et notationibus illustratum una cum glossis Gregorii XIII Pont. Max. iussu editum, 2 vols., Romae, 1582.

Denzinger, H.—Bannwart, C.—Umberg, I., *Enchiridion Symbolorum, Definitionum et Declarationum de Rebus Fidei et Morum*, 21.-23. ed., Friburgi-Brisgoviae, 1932.

Five Great Encyclicals, New York: Paulist Press, 1939.

Jaffé, P., *Regesta Pontificum Romanorum ab condita ecclesia ad annum post Christum natum MCXCVIII*, 2. ed. (F. Kaltenbrunner, P. Ewald, S. Loewenfeld), 2 vols. in 1, Lipsiae, 1885-1888.

Liber Sextus Decretalium D. Bonifatii Papae VIII suae integritati una cum Clementinis et Extravagantibus earumque Glossis restitutis, Romae, 1582.

Mansi, Ioannes, *Sacrorum Conciliorum Nova et Amplissima Collectio*, 53 vols. in 59, Parissiis-Arnhemii-Lipsiae, 1901-1927.

Potthast, A., *Regesta Pontificum Romanorum inde ab anno post Christum natum 1198 ad annum 1304*, 2 vols., Berolini, 1874-1875.

Schema Codicis Iuris Canonici, ed. cum notis Petri Card. Gasparri, Romae, 1912.

Authors

Anderson, R. G., *The Biography of a Cathedral*, New York: Longmans, Green and Co., 1946.

Augustine, Charles, *A Commentary on the New Code of Canon Law*, 8 vols., Vol. III, 2. ed., St. Louis: Herder, 1919.

Bachofen, Charles, *Compendium Juris Regularium*, Neo Eboraci, 1903.

Bakalarczyk, Richardus, *De Novitiatu*, The Catholic University of America Canon Law Studies, n. 36, Washington, D. C.: The Catholic University of America, 1927.

Berutti, C., *Institutiones Iuris Canonici*, 6 vols., Vol. III, Taurini-Romae: Marietti, 1936.

Beste, U., *Introductio in Codicem*, 3. ed., Collegeville, Minn.: St. John's Abbey Press, 1946.

Biot, R.—Galimard, P., *Guide Médical des Vocations Sacerdotales et Religieuses*, Paris, 1945.

Blat, A., *Commentarium Textus Codicis Iuris Canonici*, 5 vols. in 6, Vol. II, Pars II et III, 3. ed., Romae: Collegio Angelico, 1938.

Bouix, D., *Tractatus de Jure Regularium*, 2 vols., Parisiis, 1857.

Bouscaren, T. Lincoln—Ellis, Adam C., *Canon Law, A Text and Commentary*, Milwaukee: Bruce, 1946.

Brown, James, *The Invalidating Effects of Force, Fear, and Fraud Upon the Canonical Novitiate*, The Catholic University of America Canon Law Studies, n. 311, Washington, D. C.: The Catholic University of America, 1951.

Cappello, Felix M., *Summa Iuris Canonici*, 3 vols., Vol. I and II, 4. ed., 1945, Vol. III, 3. ed., 1948, Romae: Apud Aedes Universitatis Gregoriannae.

——————, *Tractatus Canonico-Moralis De Sacramentis*, 5 vols., Vol. IV, 2. ed., Romae: Marietti, 1947.

Carr, Aidan, *Vocation to the Priesthood: Its Canonical Concept*, The Catholic University of America Canon Law Studies, n. 293, Washington, D. C.: The Catholic University of America Press, 1950.

Carroll, P. J., *Vocations Concern All Catholics*, Notre Dame, Indiana: Ave Maria Press, 1949.

Catholic Encyclopedia, The, 15 vols., Index and 2 Supplements, New York: Appleton Co., 1907-1922.

Cocchi, G., *Commentarium in Codicem Iuris Canonici*, 8 vols. in 5, Vol. IV, 3. ed., Taurini: Marietti, 1933.

Coronata, Matthaeus, Conte a, *Institutiones Iuris Canonici ad Usum Utriusque Cleri et Scholarum*, 5 vols., Taurini, Romae: Marietti, 1936-1945; Vol. I, 2. ed., 1939.

Coussa, A., *Epitome Praelectionum de Iure Ecclesiastico Orientali*, 2 vols., Vol. II, Venetiis: Typis Polyglottis Insulae S. Lazari, 1941.

Creusen, J.—Garesché, E.—Ellis, A., *Religious Men and Women in the Code*, 4. English ed., Milwaukee: Bruce, 1942.

Delatte, P., *Commentary on the Rule of St. Benedict*, New York: Benziger, 1921.

Deroux, M., *Les Origines de l'Oblature Bénédictine*, Vienne, 1927.

Dictionnaire de Théologie Catholique, ed. A. Vacant, E. Mangenot, and E. Amann, 30 vols. incomplete, Vol. I, 3. ed., Paris: Letouzey et Ané, 1930.

Dix, Gregory, *The Treatise on the Apostolic Tradition of St. Hippolytus of Rome*, New York: The Macmillan Co., 1937.

Duffy, F., *Testing the Spirit*, St. Louis: Herder, 1948.

Eagleton, George, *The Diocesan Quinquennial Faculties Formula IV*, The Catholic University of America Canon Law Studies, n. 248, Washington, D. C.: The Catholic University of America Press, 1948.

Faherty, William, *The Destiny Of Modern Women in The Light of Papal Teaching*, Westminster, Md.: Newman, 1950.

Farrell, Edward, *The Theology of Religious Vocation*, St. Louis: B. Herder, 1951.

Freriks, Celestine, *Religious Congregations in Their External Relations*, The Catholic University Canon Law Studies, n. 1, Washington, D. C.: The Catholic University of America, 1916.

Frey, Wolfgang, *The Act of Religious Profession*, The Catholic University of America Canon Law Studies, n. 63, Washington, D. C.: The Catholic University of America, 1931.

Garrigou-Lagrange, R.—Rose, B., *The One God*, St. Louis: Herder, 1944.

Goodwine, Joseph, *The Reception of Converts*, The Catholic University Canon Law Studies, n. 198, Washington, D. C.: The Catholic University of America Press, 1944.

Goyneche, S., *Iuris Canonici Summa Principia, De Religiosis*, Romae: *Commentarium Pro Religiosis*, 1938.

Heck, T., *Christ Calls*, St. Meinrad, Indiana: St. Meinrad's Abbey Press, 1945.

Hervé, J. M., *Manuale Theologiae Dogmaticae*, 4 vols., Vol. III, 18. ed., Westminster, Md.: Newman, 1943.

Hohn, H., *Vocations, Conditions of Admission, etc., into the Convents, Congregations, Societies, Religious Institutes, According to Authentical Information and the Latest Regulations*, New York: Benziger, 1912.

————, *Vocations, Conditions of Admission, etc., into the Monasteries, Congregations, Societies, Religious Institutes, etc., According to Authentical Information and the Latest Regulations*, New York: Benziger, 1910.

Hostiensis (Henricus de Segusio), *Commentaria in Quinque Decretalium Libros*, 5 vols., in 3, Venetiis, 1581.

Jone, J.—Adelman, U., *Moral Theology*, Westminster, Md.: Newman, 1945.

Koesler, L., *Entrance into the Novitiate by Clerics in Major Orders*, The Catholic University of America Canon Law Studies, n. 327, Washington, D. C.: The Catholic University of America Press, 1952.

Kurtscheid, Bertrandus, *Historia Iuris Canonici, Historia Institutorum*, Vol. I, *Ab Ecclesiae Fundatione usque ad Gratianum*, Romae: Officium Libri Catholici, 1941.

Ladislaus a Maria Immaculata, *De Vocatione Religiosa*, Romae: Apud Studiorum Domum, 1950.

Lahitton, Joseph, *La Vocation Sacerdotale*, nouvelle edit., Paris, 1913.

Lehmkuhl, A., *Theologia Moralis*, 2 vols., 9. ed., Friburgi Brisgoviae, 1898.

McLaughlin, Terence, *Le Très Ancien Droit Monastique de l'Occident*, Paris, Abbaye Saint-Martin, 1935.

McSorley, Joseph, *Outline History of the Church by Centuries*, 4. ed., St. Louis, B. Herder, 1945.

Messenger, E. C., *Two In One Flesh*, 3 vols., London: Sands and Co., 1948.

Meyer, H.—Eckhoff, F., *The Philosophy of St. Thomas Aquinas*, St. Louis: B. Herder, 1948.

Migne, *Patrologiae Cursus Completus, Series Graeca*, 161 vols., Parisiis, 1857-1866.

————, *Patrologiae Cursus Completus, Series Latina*, 221 vols., Parisiis, 1844-1855.

Molitor, R., *Religiosi Iuris Capita Selecta*, Ratisbonae, 1909.

Montalembert, Charles, *The Monks of the West*, 2 vols., Boston, 1874.

Muzzarelli, V., *De Professione Religiosa a Primordiis ad Saeculum XII*, Romae: Apud Piam Societatem Sancti Pauli, 1938.

New Testament of Our Lord and Saviour Jesus Christ, The, Revision of the Challoner-Rheims version by the Confraternity of Christian Doctrine, Paterson, N. J., St. Anthony's Guild, 1941.

Olivero, H., *De Vocatione Religiosa Clericorum Eorumque Facultate Religionem Ingrediendi*, Romae: Apud Custodiam Librariam Pont. Instituti Utriusque Iuris, 1947.

O'Neil, F. J., *The Dismissal of Religious in Temporary Vows*, The Catholic University of America Canon Law Studies, n. 166, Washington, D. C.: The Catholic University of America Press, 1942.

Ottaviani, A., *Institutiones Iuris Publici Ecclesiastici*, 2 vols., Vol. I, 3. ed., Romae: Typis Polyglottis Vaticanis, 1947.

Orth, Clement, *The Approbation of Religious Institutes*, The Catholic University of America Canon Law Studies, n. 71, Washington, D. C.: The Catholic University of America, 1931.

Parente, Pascal, *Spiritual Direction*, St. Meinrad, Indiana: St. Meinrad's Abbey Press, 1950.

Phillips, R. P., *Modern Thomistic Philosophy*, 2 vols., Westminster, Md.: Newman, 1934.

Piat, *Compendium Iuris Regularis* (edited by Victorius ab Appeltern), Parisiis-Tornaci, 1903.

Prat, F., *La Théologie de Saint Paul*, 2 vols., Paris, 1908.

Prümmer, D., *Manuale Iuris Canonici*, 3. ed., Friburgi Brisgoviae: Herder and Co., 1922.

Ramstein, M., *A Manual of Canon Law*, Hoboken, N. J.: Terminal Printing and Publishing Co., 1948.

Regatillo, E., *Institutiones Iuris Canonici*, 2 vols., Vol. I, 2. ed., Santander: Sal Terrae, 1946.

Reiffenstuel, A., *Ius Canonicum Universum*, 5 vols. in 6, Romae, 1831-1834.

Religious Sisters, Westminster, Md.: Newman, 1950.

Rufinus, *Die Summa Decretorum des Magister Rufinus*, ed. H. Singer, Paderborn, 1902.

Schaefer, T., *De Religiosis Ad Normam Codicis Iuris Canonici*, 4. ed., Roma: Typis Polyglottis Vaticanis, 1947.

Schmalzgrueber, F., *Ius Ecclesiasticum Universum*, 5 vols. in 12, Romae, 1843-1845.

Sheed, F., *Theology and Sanity*, New York: Sheed and Ward, 1946.

Simon, A., *Guidance of Religious*, an English translation of Watterott, *Ordensleitung*, St. Louis: Herder, 1950.

Sleutjes, Michael, *Commentarius in Constitutiones Generales Fratres Minorum*, Vol. I, Ad Claras Aquas prope Florentiam, 1915.

Suarez, Franciscus, *Opera Omnia*, 26 vols. in 28, editio nova a Carolo Berton, Parisiis: Apud Ludovicum Vivès, 1856-1868.

Tanquerey, A., *Synopsis Theologiae Moralis et Pastoralis*, 3 vols., Vol. II, 10. ed., Parisiis, Tornaci, Romae: Desclée et Socii, 1936.

Tanquerey, A.—Branderis, H., *The Spiritual Life, A Treatise on Ascetical and Mystical Theology*, 2. ed., Tournai: Desclée and Co., 1930.

Thomas Aquinas, S., *Opuscula Selecta*, 4 vols., Tom. III, *Opusculum XVII*, Parisiis: Sumptibus et Typis P. Lethielleux, Editoris, 1881.

————, *Summa Theologica*, 22. ed., 6 vols., Taurini-Romae: Marietti, 1939.

Tonna-Barthet, Anthony, *The Christian Life*, New York: Pustet, 1929.

Toso, A., *Ad Codicem Juris Canonici Commentaria Minora*, 5 vols., Vol. I, 2. ed., 1921; Vols. II-V, 1922-1927, Romae: Marietti.

Van Hove, A., *Commentarium Lovaniense in Codicem Iuris Canonici*, Vol. I, Tom. I, *Prolegomena ad Codicem Iuris Canonici*, 2. ed., Mechliniae-Romae: H. Dessain, 1945.

Vermeersch, A., *De Religiosis Institutis et Personis*, 2 vols., Vol. II, 3. ed., Brugis, 1909.

————, *Religious and Ecclesiastical Vocation*, translation by J. G. Kempf, St. Louis: Herder, 1925.

Vermeersch, A.—Creusen, J., *Epitome Iuris Canonici*, 3 vols., 6. ed., Mechliniae-Romae: Dessain, 1937-1946.

Webster's International Dictionary, 2. ed., Springfield: G. & C. Merriam Co., 1948.

Wernz, F. X., *Ius Decretalium*, 2. ed., 6 vols., Romae et Prati, 1906-1913.

Wernz, F. X.—Vidal, P., *Ius Canonicum ad Codicis Normam Enactum*, 7 tomes in 8 vols., Romae: Apud Aedes Universitatis Gregorianae, 1923-1938. Tome III, 1933.

Woywod, S., *A Practical Commentary On The Code of Canon Law*, revised and enlarged edition, 2 vols., New York: John F. Wagner, 1948.

Yelle, G., *Travail Scientifique en Disciplines Ecclésiastiques*, Montréal: Grand Séminaire de Montréal, 1945.

Articles

Alston, G., "Benedict, Rule of Saint," *The Catholic Encyclopedia*, II, 436-441.

————, "Benedictine Order," *The Catholic Encyclopedia*, II, 443-465.

————, "Cluny," *The Catholic Encyclopedia*, IV, 73-74.

Anonymous, "Studia Canonica," *CpRM*, XXV (1944-1946), 57-72.

Bacdurs, F. J., "Pachomius, Saint," *The Catholic Encyclopedia*, XI, 381-382.

Bastnagel, Clement, "The Requirement of Consultation for Valid Action," *The Jurist*, IX (1949), 365-395.

Besse, J. M., "Basil, Rule of Saint," *The Catholic Encyclopedia*, II, 322-324.

Ford, Hugh, "Benedict of Nursia, Saint," *The Catholic Encyclopedia*, II, 467-472.

Hudleston, G., "Monasticism," *The Catholic Encyclopedia*, X, 459-476.

Goyeneche, S., "Studia Canonica," *CpR*, I (1920), 21-30.

Larraona, A., "Commentarium," *CpR*, I (1920), 45-50.

————, "Commentarium Codicis," *CpR*, II (1921), 134-139; 168-172.

Logar, R., "Conspectus Historico Juridicus Juris Religiosorum Orientalium," *CpRM*, XXVI (1947), 265-288.

McSorley, Joseph, "Basil The Great, Saint," *The Catholic Encyclopedia*, II, 330-334.

Stenger, Joseph, "Canonical Episcopal Visitation of Religious Communities," *The Jurist*, II (1942), Supplement.

Steiger, A. P., "De propagatione et diffusione vitae religiosae," *Periodica*, XIII (1924), (29)-(60), (73)-(100), (153)-(180).

Urrutia, "Familiae Religiosae apud Anglicanos," *CpRM*, XXVII (1948), 90-103.

Vermeersch, A., "Annotationes," *Periodica*, V (1913), 99.

————, "Annotationes," *Periodica*, VI-VII (1912-1914), 263-265.

————, "De status religiosi essentia et interpretatione can. 487 et 488," *Periodica*, XV (1926-1927), (1)-(13).

————, "Religious Life," *The Catholic Encyclopedia*, XII, 748-762.

Vromant, G., "*De signis negativis vocationis sacerdotalis et religiosae*," *Periodica*, XXII (1933), 187*-191*.

Periodicals

Commentarium pro Religiosis, Romae, 1920-1934; ab anno 1935: *Commentarium pro Religiosis et Missionariis.*

Jurist, The, Washington, D. C., 1941—

Periodica de Re Canonica et Morali utilia praesertim Religiosis et Missionariis, Brugis, 1905—

Abbreviations

AAS—Acta Apostolicae Sedis

ASS—Acta Sanctae Sedis

Bruns—*Canones Apostolorum et Consiliorum Saeculorum IV-VII.*

Bull. Rom. Taur.—Bullarium Romanum, ed. Taurinensis.

C.—Causa

c.—canon seu caput (iuris antiqui).

cc.—canones seu capita (iuris antiqui).

can.—canon (novi Codicis).

cans.—canones (novi Codicis).

Coll. Lac.—Collectio Lacensis.

Conc. Trident.—Concilium Tridentinum.

CpR(M)—Commentarium pro Religiosis (et Missionariis).

D.—Distinctio (iuris antiqui).

Fontes—Codicis Iuris Canonici Fontes, cura . . . Gasparri editi.

JE—Jaffé, *Regesta Pontificum Romanorum* (edited by P. Ewald; for the years 590-882).
JK—Jaffé, *op. cit.* (edited by F. Kaltenbrunner; to the year 590).
JL—Jaffé, *op. cit.* (edited by S. Loewenfeld; for the years 882-1198).
Mansi—Mansi, J. D., *Sacrorum Conciliorum Nova et Amplissima Collectio.*
MPG—(Migne, *Patrologia Graeca*) Migne, Jacques Paul, *Patrologiae Cursus Completus—Series Graeca.*
MPL—(Migne, *Patrologia Latina*) Migne, Jacques Paul, *Patrologiae Cursus Completus—Series Latina.*
NCWC—National Catholic Welfare Conference.
Novel.—Novellae Iustinianae.
Periodica—Periodica de Re Canonica, Morali, Liturgica.
Potthast—*Regesta Pontificum Romanorum . . .*
S.C.C.—Sacra Congregatio Concilii.
S.C. de Religiosis—Sacra Congregatio de Religiosis.
S.C. Ep. et Reg.—Sacra Congregatio Episcoporum et Regularium.
s.v.—Sub verbo; sub verbis.

BIOGRAPHICAL NOTE

NORMAN FRANCIS McFARLAND was born February 21, 1922, in Martinez, California, and received his elementary education in the public schools of that city. In September, 1935, he entered St. Joseph's College, the preparatory seminary for the Archdiocese of San Francisco. On graduation from St. Joseph's College in 1941 he entered St. Patrick's Seminary, Menlo Park, California, where he received the Bachelor of Arts Degree in June, 1943, and from which he was ordained priest on June 15, 1946. After two years of parochial work in the Archdiocese of San Francisco, he was assigned to the Catholic University of America, Washington, D. C., to pursue a course of studies in Canon Law. He received the degree of Bachelor of Canon Law in June, 1949, and the degree of Licentiate in Canon Law in June, 1950.

ALPHABETICAL INDEX

CANON LAW STUDIES*

327. KOESLER, REV. LEO J., O.S.B., J.C.L., Entrance into the Novitiate by Clerics in Major Orders (Canon 542, 2°).
328. MCFARLAND, REV. NORMAN E., A.B., J.C.L., Religious Vocation—Its Juridic Concept.
329. WIEST, REV. DONALD HERMAN, O.F.M.CAP., S.T.B., J.C.L., The Precensorship of Books.
330. DEWITT, REV. MAX GEORGE, A.B., J.C.L., The Cessation of Delegated Power.
331. MATHIS, REV. MARCIAN JOHN, O.F.M., J.C.L., The Constitution and Supreme Administration of Regional Seminaries Subject to the Sacred Congregation for the Propagation of the Faith in China.
332. SCHORR, REV. GEORGE F., A.B., J.C.L., The Law o' the Celebret.
333. SHEEHY, REV. ROBERT FRANCIS, A.B., J.C.L., The Sacred Congregation of the Sacraments: Its Competence in the Roman Curia.
334. SHIELDS, REV. JOSEPH A., A.B., J.C.L., Deprivation of the Clerical Garb.
335. URICHECK, REV. GEORGE EDWARD, A.B., J.C.L., De forma celebrationis matrimonii in Ecclesiis Orientalibus ante Motu Proprio *Crebrae Allatae* et post.
336. DEPAUW, REV. GOMMAR ALBERT LEO JULIAN MARIA, J.C.L., The Legal Status of Catholic Elementary Schools in Belgium, 1830–1950.

* For a complete list of the available numbers of this series apply to the Catholic University of America Press, 620 Michigan Avenue, N.E., Washington 17, D. C.

www.ingramcontent.com/pod-product-compliance
Lightning Source LLC
LaVergne TN
LVHW050209080826
844660LV00012B/387

* 9 7 8 0 8 1 3 2 2 4 9 9 2 *